THE OFFICIAL NAMES

OF

THE BATTLES
AND OTHER ENGAGEMENTS

FOUGHT BY

THE MILITARY FORCES OF THE BRITISH EMPIRE

DURING

THE GREAT WAR, 1914–1919,

AND

THE THIRD AFGHAN WAR, 1919.

REPORT OF THE BATTLES NOMENCLATURE COMMITTEE AS
APPROVED BY THE ARMY COUNCIL.

The Naval & Military Press Ltd

Published by

The Naval & Military Press Ltd
Unit 5 Riverside, Brambleside
Bellbrook Industrial Estate
Uckfield, East Sussex
TN22 1QQ England

Tel: +44 (0)1825 749494

www.naval-military-press.com
www.nmarchive.com

In reprinting in facsimile from the original, any imperfections are inevitably reproduced and the quality may fall short of modern type and cartographic standards.

FOREWORD.

By Colonel Terry Cave.

Two years ago the London Stamp Exchange issued a reprint of E. A. James's *'Record of the Battles and Engagements of the British Armies in France and Flanders 1914–1918,'* an invaluable little work of reference whose reappearance, after more than sixty five years, has been well received. Now, the L.S.E. has made another, even more significant contribution to the material available for the study of the Great War—the first reprint of the Battles Nomenclature Committee Report, the report on which James's booklet was based.

This most important document was originally published seventy years ago and has long since disappeared from general view and yet it remains an essential source for historians and students alike. Indeed it is unique in that it is the sole authority for what action fought during the Great War and the Afghan War of 1919 has official recognition, under what name it is known and what are its geographical and chronological limits. It covers every theatre of war from the Western Front to China, and it provides the framework on which the history of that conflict has been and continues to be written. It was also the basis on which the regiments laid claim to their battle honours.

The Committee, on which Australia, Canada, New Zealand and South Africa were permanently represented and India and the Colonies on an as-required basis, assembled in August 1919 under the chairmanship of Major General Sir John Emerson Wharton Headlam. Sir John was a gunner who, between 1914 and 1916, had served successively as C.R.A. 5th Infantry Division, M.G.R.A. Second Army, and M.G.R.A. G.H.Q. B.E.F. Subsequently, in January 1917, he had accompanied Lord Milner as his artillery expert on the Inter-Allied Mission to Russia, and the following year he had headed the Artillery Mission to the U.S.A. This nomenclature committee was his last assignment before retiring in 1921.

The results of the Committee's deliberations are laid out in tabular form in the second part of the report and in themselves provide a diary of the war, theatre by theatre. With one or two minor exceptions, the document is solely concerned with land operations involving British and Empire forces.

But although these tables are the essence of the report, the first part, which addresses the terms of reference, makes absorbing reading. Here is the reasoning behind the Committee's decisions; here are explained the principles it followed in devising the system of classification of engagements. Firepower and numbers engaged alone could not always be the predominant factors in deciding the relative importance of engagements, moral and political effects of an action had also to be considered. As the report points out, an action that in terms of the fighting on the Western Front might have been regarded as a local affair, in some minor theatre might have had an effect out of all proportion to the numbers engaged and due weight had to be given to that outcome.

There was certainly one problem facing the Committee, and one they could do nothing about: the events they were studying had happened so recently that there were very few authoritative documents published to which they could refer. This in turn led to some decisions that might have been different had the Committee had the time and source material at their disposal; but as far as the authorities were concerned speed was of the essence. Some changes were approved later when the War Office announced the list of Battles Honours; E. A. James quotes "Battle of Pozières Ridge" becoming "Battle of Pozières" as an example.

There are areas of disagreement. The official titles "The Battles of Ypres 1914, 1915 and 1917" are commonly replaced, even by historians, with "First, Second and Third Ypres." The Official History notes the impossibility of adhering to the geographical limits fixed by the Committee when it [the Official History] describes the fighting round Ypres in October/November 1914. It also takes issue with the decision to fix the end of the Battle of Loos as 8 Oct 1915 and so exclude what the Committee refers to as the "Actions of the Hohenzollern Redoubt." These took place between 9 and 13 Oct and as far as the Official History is concerned are part of the Battle of Loos.

Despite such comparatively minor points of difference, this is a valuable and essential document, and its reissue is an important step in the process of making out-of-print, official material widely available to the increasing number of students of the history of the Great War.

Terry Cave,
Worthing, April 1992.

ARMY.

THE OFFICIAL NAMES

OF

THE BATTLES

AND OTHER ENGAGEMENTS

FOUGHT BY

THE MILITARY FORCES OF THE BRITISH EMPIRE

DURING

THE GREAT WAR, 1914-1919,

AND

THE THIRD AFGHAN WAR, 1919.

REPORT OF THE BATTLES NOMENCLATURE COMMITTEE AS APPROVED BY THE ARMY COUNCIL.

Presented to Parliament by Command of His Majesty.

LONDON:
PUBLISHED BY HIS MAJESTY'S STATIONERY OFFICE.

To be purchased through any Bookseller or directly from
H.M. STATIONERY OFFICE at the following addresses:
IMPERIAL HOUSE, KINGSWAY, LONDON, W.C.2, and 28, ABINGDON STREET, LONDON, S.W.1;
37, PETER STREET, MANCHESTER; 1, ST. ANDREW'S CRESCENT, CARDIFF;
or 23, FORTH STREET, EDINBURGH.

1922.

[Cmd. 1138.] *Price* 2/- *Net.*

CONTENTS.

	PAGE
Terms of Reference..	3
Constitution of Committee..	3
Procedure—	
Documentary evidence ..	4
Personal evidence	5
Definition of limits—	
Chronological	5
Geographical	5
Classification of engagements	6
Subdivision of battles	6
Terminology	7
Nomenclature	7
Conclusion ..	8

TABULATED LIST OF ENGAGEMENTS.

(Arranged according to Theatres of War.)

		PAGE
France and Flanders..		12
Italy ..		26
Macedonia		27
Dardanelles ..		28
Egypt and Palestine ..	*Sudan* ..	30
	Western Frontier	30
	Eastern Frontier and Palestine	31
Arabia..	*Hejaz* ..	34
	Southern Arabia	35
Mesopotamia ..		36
Persia and Central Asia	*South Persia and the Persian Gulf* ..	40
	East Persia and Trans-Caspia	42
	North-West Persia and the Caspian ..	43
India ..	*North-West Frontier and Baluchistan*	44
	The Third Afghan War	46
	North-East Frontier and Burma	47
Russia ..	*Murman*	48
	Archangel	50
	Siberia ..	52
Far East and Pacific..	*China* ..	53
	Australasia	53
East Africa		54
South-West Africa ..		60
West Africa ..	*Togo* ..	61
	French West Africa .	61
	Cameroons	62

The cost of this Committee is 599*l*., of which 126*l*. represents the cost of printing and publishing the Report.

REPORT.

Terms of Reference.
1. The "Battles Nomenclature Committee" was appointed in August, 1919, the Terms of Reference being:—

"(*a.*) To tabulate the actions fought in this war.
"(*b.*) To classify these actions with a definite system of nomenclature which will
" denote their relative importance (*e.g.*, the more important actions might
" be classed as battles, and the lesser ones as combats, &c.).
"(*c.*) To define the geographical and chronological limits of each action."

Constitution of Committee.
2. The following list shows all officers who have served on the Committee. It will be seen that circumstances unfortunately necessitated several changes, but the consequent inconvenience was minimized as much as possible by arranging for overlaps.

PRESIDENT.

Major-General Sir John Headlam, K.B.E., C.B., D.S O.

PERMANENT MEMBERS.

Appointed by the General Staff:—

Captain G. C. FitzH. Harcourt-Vernon, D.S.O., Grenadier Guards, 13th to 21st August.
Lieut.-Colonel P. R. Worrall, D.S.O., M.C., Devonshire Regiment. 25th August to date.

Australian Representatives:—

Brigadier-General C. H. Jess, C.M.G., D.S.O., Australian Imperial Force. 18th to 20th August.
Lieut.-Colonel J. L. Whitham, C.M.G., D.S.O., Australian Imperial Force, 19th August to 7th October and from 31st November to 16th January.
Colonel R. Dowse, D.S.O., Australian Imperial Force, 7th October to 2nd January.
Lieut.-Colonel G. C. Somerville, C.M.G., D.S.O., Australian Imperial Force, 26th to 30th January.
Lieut.-Colonel E. C. Plant, D.S.O., O.B.E., Australian Imperial Force, 9th February to date.

Canadian Representatives:—

Brigadier-General J. H. MacBrien, C.B., C.M.G., D.S.O., Military Forces of Canada, 18th to 20th August.
Lieut.-Colonel T. M. McAvity, C.B.E., D.S.O., Military Forces of Canada, 17th August to date.
Major C. W. Erlebach O.B.E., Military Forces of Canada, 6th November to date.

New Zealand Representatives:—

Colonel H. Stewart, C.M.G., D.S.O., M.C., New Zealand Military Forces, 18th to 20th August.
Brigadier-General G. N. Johnson, C.M.G., D.S.O., New Zealand Military Forces, 1st September.
Major H. S. Westmacott, O.B.E., Auckland Regiment, 3rd to 5th September.
Captain A. H. H. Lewis, Otago Regiment 3rd September to date.

South African Representatives:—

Lieut.-Colonel G. Helbert, C.B.E., South African Military Forces, 18th and 19th August, and 21st October to date.
Major H. P. Mills, O.B.E., South African Military Forces, 20th August to 10th October.

Temporary Members.

(Appointed by the General Staff.)

France and Flanders:—
Lieut.-Colonel B. W. B. Bowdler, C.M.G., D.S.O., Royal Engineers
Lieut.-Colonel W. G. S. Dobbie, D.S.O., Royal Engineers.[*]

Italy:—
Colonel G. W. Howard, C.M.G., D.S.O., Essex Regiment.
Lieut.-Colonel J. E. Turner, C.M.G., D.S.O., Scottish Rifles.

Macedonia:—
Lieut.-Colonel E. G. L. Thurlow, D.S.O., Somerset Light Infantry.
Lieut.-Colonel A. P. Blackwood, D.S.O., Border Regiment.

Dardanelles:—
Lieut.-Colonel J. E. F. d'Apice, D.S.O., Royal Artillery.
Major F. L. G. West, Auckland Regiment.

Egypt and Palestine:—
Lieut.-Colonel A. E. M. Sinclair Thompson, D.S.O., Essex Regiment.
Major J. A. H. Gammell, D.S.O., M.C., Royal Artillery.

Mesopotamia:—
Lieut.-Colonel R. N. Dick, C.M.G., D.S.O., Royal Sussex Regiment.
Lieut.-Colonel W. E. Wilson-Johnston, C.I.E., D.S.O., 36th Sikhs.

Persia and India:—
Colonel E. F. Orton, 37th Lancers.
Lieut.-Colonel C. W. G. Walker, D.S.O., 37th Dogras.

Secretaries.

(Appointed from the Historical Section, Committee of Imperial Defence.)
Captain C. T. Atkinson, O.U.O.T.C., 18th August to 19th September.
Captain H. Fitz M. Stacke, M.C., Worcestershire Regiment, 13th August to date.
Lieut. S. R. P. Roberts, Royal Sussex Regiment, (*Assistant Secretary*) 26th January to 30th June.

The temporary members mentioned above were appointed to assist the Committee in the consideration of particular campaigns, being specially selected for their local knowledge. For the other theatres of war temporary members were not appointed, but assistance was obtained as required from officers who had served in the campaign under consideration.

Procedure. 3. The Committee met on Monday, 18th August, 1919, and the first session was devoted to a general consideration of the scope of the work, an examination of the correspondence on the subject, and a discussion of the principles to be followed. The various campaigns were then studied in detail with the aid of both documentary and personal evidence.

Documentary evidence.—The Committee have carefully examined all the Despatches and Reports, whether published or unpublished, which have been placed at their disposal by the War, Colonial, and India Offices, and also the "Diary of the War" compiled by the Historical Section of the Committee of Imperial Defence, so far as it has been completed. They have received valuable assistance from the Headquarters of the different Dominion Forces and from the Admiralty, and many accounts published unofficially have also been read and considered in Committee. In all matters of doubt the War Diaries have been freely consulted, and the Committee are under great

---
[*] Relieved on account of other duties.

obligations to the Historical Section of the Committee of Imperial Defence for their help in this and other matters, and for placing a room at their disposal.

The Committee wish also to take this opportunity of placing on record their appreciation of the work of the officers of that section who acted as their secretaries. They are particularly indebted to them for able memoranda on the principles and practice of nomenclature and classification.

Personal evidence.—To supplement the documentary evidence, the Committee have taken full advantage of the permission given to them to call upon individual officers with special knowledge for their assistance. In most cases these officers attended meetings of the Committee and took part in the discussions, and several were good enough to describe the course of particular campaigns in lectures. At an early meeting the Committee decided that the evidence of these officers should not be recorded. In coming to this decision the Committee were prompted by two main considerations. In the first place, they felt that they would be able to obtain a better idea of the actual circumstances by informal discussion than by formal evidence. In the second, they considered that only in such a way could they obtain the benefit of hearing the views of officers of high rank without abrogating their own responsibility for their recommendations.

Definition of limits. 4. Of the various tasks allotted to the Committee in their terms of reference, the definition of the limits of engagements, both geographical and chronological, has been the simplest.

As regards *chronological* limits it was decided—

That no attempt should be made to define the time more closely than by the "day" (midnight to midnight).

That, owing to the varying length of the preparatory action, and the difficulty of fixing its actual commencement, this period should not be included, but that "zero day" should be taken as the first day in all cases.

That, on the other hand, the period of consolidation after an attack should, as a general rule, be included.

As regards *geographical* limits the Committee decided to denote the boundaries of battle areas by easily recognizable geographical features which could be followed on such generally accessible maps as those of the 1/100,000 series. In doing so they have been influenced by the conviction that, for the purposes of this Committee, a meticulous accuracy was of less importance than that their recommendations should be generally intelligible without the use of special maps.

The general principle followed has been to include in a battle area only what might fairly be regarded as the actual "battlefield." With the great range of modern guns any attempt to comprise in this all positions occupied by our artillery engaged,* or all ground covered by the enemy's shell fire, would unduly extend the limits. For the rear line, the geographical feature approximating most closely to the main line of the heavy artillery has been taken, but the flanks have been fixed to correspond with the outside limits from which the infantry assault was delivered, or within which the enemy's infantry advanced to the attack. The above, of course, applies especially to trench warfare, but the same principles have been applied as far as practicable to engagements in the open.

In certain cases it has been found impossible to define the limits more closely than by the expressions "beyond" a certain line or base, or "in the neighbourhood of" a certain place. The use of such means of definition has, however, been confined to cases where it is thought that no doubt can arise as to the troops concerned. Where there has been a danger of this occurring, as, for instance, in rear-guard actions where the main body had passed over the same ground on the same day, formations have been named. Otherwise, the indication of the troops engaged has been strictly avoided as being beyond the province of the Committee.

---

* The Committee consider, however, that it should be definitely accepted that all batteries firing upon the front of attack should be held to have taken part in the engagement.

As regards *subsidiary actions*, the Committee decided that any which took place outside the geographical limits laid down as above for the main battle, should be considered on their merits as separate engagements. In cases, however, where such engagements were definitely undertaken as contributing to the battle, this has been indicated.

Classification of engagements.

5. It is in devising a system of classification which would be generally applicable that the Committee have been confronted with the most difficult problem. This is due, of course, to the very different conditions prevailing in the different theatres of war. If a scale suitable for some of the minor theatres had been strictly applied to the Western Front, it would have involved an innumerable list of "raids" and similar minor operations. If the process had been reversed, it would have meant omitting all mention of any but one or two actions in wars of some years' duration. It must always be remembered that if the actual fighting in other campaigns never reached the intensity of the great battles in France and Belgium, the troops who took part in them enjoyed none of the amenities due to a European environment; they had to undergo privations of food and ordeals of climate for long periods without any chance of relief; and they suffered in some cases very severely from the depressing effects of disease. They would have real cause for disappointment if their fights were denied a place in the roll of engagements as being mere skirmishes in comparison with the great struggles in the West.

Moreover, in judging of the importance of military action, due weight must be given to the moral and political effect at the time. Engagements may have a far-reaching influence out of all proportion to the number of troops engaged. To go further, success or failure in the defence of some frontier post—insignificant by European standards—may well be the decisive factor in determining the attitude of the inhabitants of vast regions, and thus affect the whole course of the subsequent campaign.

The Committee came early to the conclusion that any attempt to classify the engagements in all the theatres of war on hard-and-fast rules based on the numbers engaged, the casualties suffered, or any similar foundation must work unfairly in practice. The principles they have followed in their classification are explained in the following paragraphs.

Subdivision of battles.

6. The extension of the period covered by the so-called battles in Europe from days to weeks, and even to months, has introduced an entirely new factor, and the term "battle" in the ordinary pre-war application of that word is obviously no longer sufficient. From the despatches it is plain that the Commander-in-Chief's conception of such operations as the so-called "Battle of the Somme" (1916) was a *series of great blows*, each delivered with the full force available, after the necessary pause for preparation. The Committee have endeavoured to present them in this form by resolving them into their successive stages:—first the main attack—then the succeeding general attacks marking the opening of new phases. Each of these constitutes in itself a "Battle" of the first magnitude, and the whole operation thus comes to form a Group of Battles.* This is, after all, only a parallel to the changes in organization. The expansion in the size of the field armies has necessitated their subdivision, not only into Armies, but into "Groups of Armies." We spoke of the "British Armies" in France, not of the "British Army," so we may speak of the "Battles of the Somme" rather than of the "Battle of the Somme." This principle has accordingly been followed by the Committee in all such cases. Historical sanction for this usage is not wanting. Wellington's operations on the French frontier in 1813 were grouped by Napier under the title of the "Battles of the Pyrenees," and half a century later, in the American Civil War, we have the "Battles of the Wilderness."

Even with this arrangement, many of the individual battles will still be on so grand a scale that the Committee have seriously considered the possibility of further subdivision by *breaking up the front* of the great simultaneous attacks and denominating the struggle for each distinctive feature a separate battle. This would no doubt appeal to many units—from corps to battalions—to whom a battle fought on a wide front often means only the fighting for some definite locality. The Committee have the greatest sympathy with such feelings, and have always been anxious to give due regard to them, but it is their duty to consider the commanders who planned as well as

---

* Compare the French official term "Bataille d'ensemble."

the units who executed, and any such subdivision of the front is liable to give a false impression as regards the unity of the plan. It would be misleading if such attacks as those of the 1st July, 1916, and the 31st July, 1917, were represented as a series of disjointed actions. Moreover, to name even all the villages which were scenes of desperate conflicts would carry such subdivision beyond all reason. Thus at once would arise the risk of injustice to those units who fought just as gallantly for less prominent localities, or for some nameless trench.

The Committee, therefore, decided that battles fought under a single plan on a continuous front should not be broken up, but should each constitute a separate battle. At the same time, they have mentioned some of the more important tactical incidents of the battles when this could be done without risk of obscuring the greater issues involved. It must not, however, be inferred that the fighting at the places named was necessarily more severe than on other parts of the front, or that the number of such incidents recorded is any criterion of the greatness of the battle itself.

Terminology.

7. As regards the terms to be employed in describing the different engagements, the Committee have had great difficulty in arriving at any system which would adequately cover the very wide range required.

The only names in the military terminology which convey any real indication of proportion are "battle," "action," and "affair," and these are obviously inadequate to convey all the graduations. As explained above, the Committee decided to supplement them by adopting the plural—"Battles"—for those *prolonged operations* which were such a feature of the later stages of the war on the Western Front. Even with this addition a gap was still left, for there were no means of differentiating between battles so different in size as, say, Messines and Ctesiphon. The Committee carefully considered the possibility of recommending the use of some such term as "super-battle" or "battle-royal"* to denote those battles which did not come within the category of "groups of battles," but were yet vastly greater in scale than any single "battle" of the past. It was felt, however, that the objections to such compounds outweighed any technical advantage that might be gained by their use.

In the use of the above terms, and also of what may be called *descriptive* terms, such as "capture," "occupation," "attack," "defence," &c., the Committee have endeavoured to maintain a certain consistency. Thus the rank of "battle" has been confined as a general rule to engagements of primary importance fought out between forces not smaller than the corps. The title "action" has been employed for the next class, the limit in this case being taken as the division; lesser engagements have been styled "affairs." The term "combat" has been avoided as having reverted to its original use of a hand-to-hand fight between individuals, and so become obsolete in the sense in which it was employed in the last century. "Capture" has been reserved for operations where the primary object was the capture of a definite locality, and where this was only accomplished by actual fighting of some importance; where this latter condition was absent "occupation" has been used, and the same distinction has been drawn between "passage" and "crossing." Again the term "attack" has been confined to unsuccessful offensive operations, and "defence" to successful defences of definite localities, the term "German (or other) attack" being used in cases of simple resistance to an attack. In some cases the Committee have made use of the expedient of combination to give recognition to the cumulative effect of a series of small collisions where—as often in bush fighting—a number of these have taken the place of a pitched battle.

These and other rules which have been formulated from time to time by the Committee have, however, been intended only as general guides in applying the terms available, and they have not hesitated to depart from them where such a course appeared to be justified by the circumstances. The proportion of the troops engaged to the whole force in the field has been taken into account; moral and political effect has been considered; and the prescriptive right acquired by some engagements which have seized the popular imagination to higher titles than are strictly warranted has been recognized.

Nomenclature.

8. The great extension of the battle fronts has brought with it peculiar difficulties in deciding on appropriate names. "Double-barrelled" names† have been freely used in despatches and in official accounts, and had, no doubt,

---

* Compare the old German term "Kaiserschlacht."   † Such as "Ypres—Armentieres."

many advantages *at the moment*. But the Committee can find no sanction for such a system in the practice of English historians, or among the Battle Honours of British Regiments. Even when officially adopted abroad, as in "Gravelotte—St. Privat," such double names appear to have dropped out of popular usage.

It is true that no battles fought by the British Army in the past have been at all on the same scale as some of those under consideration. Many of the older battles, however, were fought over fronts of several miles which included more than one locality of importance, so that the use of double names could have been justified in their case by the same arguments as now apply. But in each case one name appears to have been selected, and the Committee consider that this is the only course likely to ensure the general adoption of the official names. They are aware that their choice has often been quite arbitrary, but it has never been made without the fullest consideration of all suggested alternatives.

In cases where several battles have been fought over the same ground and must obviously bear the same name, as in the case of the four successive "Battles of Ypres," the Committee came early to the conclusion that it was better to distinguish them by the year in which they were fought than to number them—to speak of "Ypres 1915" rather than of "Second Ypres." The advantage of this course is well exemplified by the case of the Battles of the Aisne. Three great battles were fought on the same stretch of that river, in 1914, 1917, and 1918, but only in the first and third of these did British troops bear a part. For us to designate the battle in 1918 the "Second Battle of the Aisne" (as it was so far as British troops were concerned) would lead to confusion since the French have officially entitled it the "Third Battle." For us to call it the "Third Battle" would be equally misleading. "Aisne 1918" solves the difficulty.

The Committee considered the possibility of using "date-names" in some cases in which it was particularly difficult to decide on the most appropriate geographical designation as, for instance, for the opening attack in the Battles of the Somme, 1916, or the initial blow of the great German offensive in 1918. Careful examination of historical precedent, however, proves that dates, although frequently used in contemporary writings, have not persisted in practice, but have always been replaced eventually by "local" names.* The Committee are of opinion that "1st July" and "21st March," however familiar now, will not convey the same meaning to future generations, and they have decided not to recommend any such titles.

The fact that in so many theatres we were fighting alongside troops of the Allied armies has introduced some complications. Full use has been made of the information supplied by the Allied Military Missions as regards the names officially adopted abroad, and where detachments from the British Army were fighting as portions of the army of one of the Allies, as on the Marne and Aisne in 1918, and in Italy, the names approved by the nation chiefly concerned have been adopted. The Committee consider, however, that for the battles *in which the British Armies in France took a major part*, official adoption of the names which have become familiar to the British public, as well as to the troops, is essential. For instance, to call the Battle of Loos "The Third Battle of Artois" would be impossible.

The nomenclature adopted by the enemy has also been noted.

With regard to the spelling of place-names, the Committee have throughout been guided by the advice of the inter-departmental Permanent Committee on Geographical Names†, to whom they are greatly indebted for continual assistance. In a few cases the general system has been departed from, in order to retain a conventional form which has become generally familiar.

Conclusion. 9. A tabulated list of the engagements fought during the War, classified, and with their geographical and chronological limits defined as directed, is attached.

As a general rule no reference has been made to the work of the Navy or Air Force, or to Allied troops fighting in line with our own. In some few cases, however, where the other forces have been small, and where the co-operation has been very close, their engagements have been included.

By an arrangement in several columns, by the use of different terms and of varieties of type, the Committee have endeavoured to indicate the relative importance of events, in accordance with the principles explained in the preceding paragraphs. It is fully recognized that many cases may be found which are not entirely in accord with these principles. The Committee believe, however, that any attempt to apply hard and fast rules to such a

---

* Except in a few cases of *Naval* battles.
† Meeting at the headquarters of the Royal Geographical Society.

complex subject would result in much greater inconsistencies, and would, moreover, in many cases be unjust. The members of the Committee have themselves had very varied experiences during the war; they have had access to the official documents as well as the assistance of a large number of officers specially qualified to speak on the subject; they have carefully considered each case in all its aspects, and they believe that their recommendations do substantial justice.

JOHN HEADLAM, *Major-General*,
President.

R. DOWSE, *Colonel*,*
G. HELBERT, *Lieut.-Colonel*,
PERCY R. WORRALL, *Lieut.-Colonel.*
J. L. WHITHAM, *Lieut.-Colonel*,
E. C. PLANT, *Lieut.-Colonel*,
MALCOLM McAVITY, *Lieut.-Colonel*,
C. W. ERLEBACH, *Major*,
A. H. LEWIS, *Captain.*
} *Members.*

H. FITZ M. STACKE, *Captain*,
Secretary.

9th July, 1920.

---

* Unfortunately, Colonel Dowse had to return to Australia before the final session of the Committee. This Report had, however, been drafted before he left and the draft was signed by him. The final Report is substantially the same as that draft and his signature has therefore, with his agreement, been appended to it.

TABULATED LIST OF ENGAGEMENTS.

NOTES.

The "Operations" column is intended to give a general outline of the course of events, and thus form a guide to the list of engagements given in the columns following.

In the "Geographical Limits" column, when no road, river, or other geographical feature is mentioned, the limit must be understood to be a straight line between the localities named. These latter are always "inclusive" unless the contrary is stated. An asterisk indicates that no more exact definition of the battle-area can be given than that the engagement took place "in the neighbourhood of" the place named.

FRANCE AND FLANDERS.

I.—THE GERMAN INVASION, 1914.

OPERATIONS.	BATTLES.		TACTICAL INCIDENTS INCLUDED.	ACTIONS, &c.	MISCELLANEOUS INCIDENTS.	LIMITS.	
	NAME.					CHRONOLOGICAL.	GEOGRAPHICAL.
The Retreat from Mons (23rd August–5th September, 1914.)	...		...	...	...	23rd August – 5th September	North of the Seine, and east of the road Paris — Roye — Péronne — Cambrai — Valenciennes—Condé.
	BATTLE OF MONS		...	—with subsidiary Action of Elouges	...	23rd–24th August	The river d'Estinne to Peissant : thence a line to Rouveroy—Quévy-le-Petit— Athis — Quiévrechain — Condé (exclusive).
				Rearguard Action of Solesmes	...	24th August	
					...	25th August	Between the rivers St. Georges and d'Erclin, north of the line Saleeches—Soleannes— St. Vaast.
	BATTLE OF LE CATEAU		...	Affair of Landrecies	...	25th August	*
					...	26th August	Basuel (exclusive)—St. Souplet— Walincourt—Esnes.
				Rearguard Affair of le Grand Fayt	...	26th August	Neighbourhood of the villages of Marbaix and le Grand Fayt, and the ground between them.
				Rearguard Affair of Etreux	...	27th August	Neighbourhood of the villages of Fesmy and Etreux, and the ground between them.
				Affair of Cerizy	...	28th August	*
				Affair of Néry	...	1st September	*
				Rearguard Action of Crépy-en-Valois	...	1st September	North of Crépy-en-Valois.
				Rearguard Actions of Villers Cotterets	...	1st September	(a.) Near Taillefontaine. (b.) In the forest north of Villers Cotterets. (c.) Near Pisseleux.

13

The Advance to the Aisne (6th September–1st October, 1914.)	BATTLE OF THE MARNE, 1914†	Passage of the Petit Morin Passage of the Marne	...	7th–10th September	Château-Thierry — La Ferté-Gaucher — th river Grand Morin to Crécy ; thence a line to Dhuisy.
	BATTLE OF THE AISNE, 1914†	Passage of the Aisne and Capture of the Aisne Heights, including the Chemin des Dames.	—*with subsequent*— (i.) Actions on the Aisne Heights	12th–15th September	Onlches — Maizy — Blanzy — Septmonts Soissons—Crouy—Alleman.
				20th September	North of the Aisne, between Paissy and Vailly (*exclusive*).
			(ii.) Action of Chivy	26th September	North of the Aisne, between Troyon and Beaulne.
The Defence of Antwerp (4th–10th October, 1914.)	...	...	...	4th–10th October	
Operations in Flanders, 1914 (10th October—22nd November.)	BATTLE OF LA BASSÉE	...	...	10th October – 2nd November	Road Noyelles-lez-Vermelles — Beuvry — Béthune (*exclusive*)—Estaires (*exclusive*) : thence a line to Fournes (*exclusive*).
	BATTLE OF MESSINES, 1914	...	...	12th October – 2nd November	The river Douve from Warneton to Dranoutre ; thence a line to Caestre Station—Abeele Station—Reninghelst—Dickebusch—Voormezeele : thence along the Canal.
	BATTLE OF ARMENTIÈRES	Capture of Meteren	...	13th October – 2nd November	Fournes — Estaires — Hazebrouck Station — Caestre Station — Dranoutre (*exclusive*) : thence the river Douve.
	THE BATTLES OF YPRES, 1914			19th October–22nd November.	The Comines Canal to Ypres : thence the Yser Canal to Steenstraat : from there the road to Bixschoote and, thence along the southern edge of the Houthulst Forest.
	(i.) BATTLE OF LANGEMARCK, 1914	...	...	21st–24th October	
	(ii.) BATTLE OF GHELUVELT	...	...	29th–31st October	
	(iii.) BATTLE OF NONNE BOSSCHEN	...	...	11th November	

† The tactical incidents and limits given for these battles refer only to the operations of the British troops engaged.

FRANCE AND FLANDERS—continued.

II.—TRENCH WARFARE, 1914-16.

OPERATIONS.	BATTLES.		ACTIONS, &c.	MISCELLANEOUS INCIDENTS.	LIMITS.	
	NAME.	TACTICAL INCIDENTS INCLUDED.			CHRONOLOGICAL.	GEOGRAPHICAL.
Winter Operations, 1914-15 (November-February.)	...	...	Defence of Festubert	...	23rd-24th November	Givenchy (exclusive)—Gorre: thence road to le Touret—Rue de l'Epinette—la Quinque Rue.
			Attack on Wytschaete	...	14th December	Road Wytschaete—Lindenhoek—Mt. Kemmel—la Clytte—Hallebast—Vierstraat—Wytschaete.
			Defence of Givenchy, 1914	...	20th-21st December	The la Bassée Canal to Gorre: thence road to le Touret—Rue de l'Epinette—la Quinque Rue.
			First Action of Givenchy, 1915	...	25th January	Road la Bassée—Annequin—Beuvry—Gorre—Festubert (exclusive).
			Affairs of Cuinchy	...	29th January, 1st and 6th February	Between the road and canal from Beuvry to la Bassée.
Summer Operations, 1915 (March-October.)	BATTLE OF NEUVE CHAPELLE	...	...	...	10th-13th March	Road Richebourg-l'Avoué—Croix Barbée—Pont du Hem—Fauquissart—Aubers.
			Action of St. Eloi	...	14th-15th March	*
			Capture of Hill 60	...	17th-22nd April	The Comines—Ypres railway as far as Zillebeke Lake, and thence the Zillebeke—Klein Zillebeke road.
	THE BATTLES OF YPRES, 1915		...	...	22nd April-25th May	
	(i.) BATTLE OF GRAVENSTAFEL RIDGE	The Gas Attack	...	...	22nd-23rd April	The Comines—Ypres Canal as far as Voormezeele: thence road to Vlamertinghe Château—Elverdinghe Château—Boesinghe—Langemarck.
	(ii.) BATTLE OF ST. JULIEN	...	...	...	24th April-4th May	
	(iii.) BATTLE OF FREZENBERG RIDGE	...	...	...	8th-13th May	
	(iv.) BATTLE OF BELLEWAARDE RIDGE	...	...	...	24th-25th May	

BATTLE OF AUBERS RIDGE	Attack at Fromelles	...	9th May	Road Aubers—Fauquissart—Laventie—Rouge-de-Bout—Fleurbaix (exclusive)—la Boutillerie—Bas Maisnil.
BATTLE OF FESTUBERT	Attack at Rue du Bois	...		Road la Quinque Rue (exclusive)—le Touret—Lacouture—Croix Barbée: thence a line to the Bois du Biez (South-West Corner).
	...	...	15th–25th May	The la Bassée Canal to Gorre; thence road to le Touret.— Lacouture — Croix Barbée: thence a line to the Bois du Biez (South-West Corner).
	...	Second Action of Givenchy, 1915	15th–16th June	Givenchy—Gorre; thence road to le Touret—Rue de l'Epinette—la Quinque Rue (exclusive).
	...	First Attack on Bellewaerde	16th June	Gheluvelt — Zillebeke : thence road to Ypres (exclusive)—Zonnebeke.
	...	Actions of Hooge	19th and 30th July and 9th August	Gheluvelt — Zillebeke : thence road to Ypres (exclusive)—Zonnebeke.
THE BATTLE OF LOOS	...	...	25th September–8th October	Road Air-Noulette — Noeux-les-Mines — Béthune (exclusive)—Gorre—Festubert (exclusive).
		—with subsidiary (i.) Action of Piètre	25th September	Haut Pommereau — Neuve Chapelle (exclusive)—Rouge Croix—Pont du Hem—l'Epinette—Aubers.
		(ii.) Action of Bois Grenier	25th September	Bas Maisnil — Croix-Maréchal — Bac-St.-Maur—Erquinghem—Bois Grenier—Bois Blancs.
		(iii.) Second Attack on Bellewaerde	25th–26th September	Gheluvelt — Zillebeke : thence road to Ypres (exclusive)—Zonnebeke.
		—and subsequent Actions of the Hohenzollern Redoubt	13th–19th October	Road Hulluch — Loos — Fosse No. 7 — Noyelles-lez-Vermelles—Cambrin.
Local Operations, 1916†	...	Actions of The Bluff	14th–15th February and 2nd March	Between the Ypres—Comines Canal and the Ypres—Comines railway (Ypres exclusive).
	...	Actions of St. Eloi Craters	27th March – 16th April	Road Wytschaete — Vierstraat — Ypres (exclusive) : thence the Ypres—Comines railway.
	...	German Attack on Vimy Ridge	21st May	Thélus—Neuville-St. Vaast—Mont-St.-Eloy —Carency—Ablain-St. Nazaire : thence along the Notre-Dame-de-Lorette ridge to the river Souchez.
BATTLE OF MOUNT SORREL	...	...	2nd–13th June	Between the Ypres—Comines Canal and the Ypres—Roulers railway (Ypres exclusive).

† Previous to the Allied Offensive.

FRANCE AND FLANDERS—continued.

III.—THE ALLIED OFFENSIVE, 1916.

OPERATIONS.	BATTLES.		ACTIONS, &c.	MISCELLANEOUS INCIDENTS.	LIMITS.	
	NAME.	TACTICAL INCIDENTS INCLUDED.			CHRONOLOGICAL.	GEOGRAPHICAL.
Operations on the Somme (1st July–18th November, 1916.)	THE BATTLES OF THE SOMME, 1916	...	...	...	1st July–18th November	
	(i.) BATTLE OF ALBERT, 1916	Capture of Montauban Capture of Mametz Capture of Fricourt Capture of Contalmaison Capture of la Boisselle		...	1st–13th July	The Combles valley to Hardecourt: thence the road to Maricourt—Susanne—Bray—Albert—Bouzincourt—Hédauville—Forceville—Bertrancourt—Sailly-au-Bois (exclusive)—Hébuterne—Puisieux-au-Mont.
			—with subsidiary Attack on the Gommecourt Salient	...	1st July	Road Puisieux-au-Mont — Hébuterne — Sailly-au-Bois — Bayencourt — Souastre — Humbercamps — Pommier — Berles-au-Bois—Monchy-au-Bois.
	(ii.) BATTLE OF BAZENTIN RIDGE	Capture of Longueval Capture of Trônes Wood Capture of Ovillers	...	...	14th–17th July	Road Hardecourt—Maricourt—Fricourt—Bécourt—Albert (exclusive): thence the river Ancre.
			—with subsidiary Attack at Fromelles	...	19th July	Road Aubers—Fauquissart—Laventie—Rouge-de-Bout—Fleurbaix (exclusive)—la Boutillerie—Bas Maisnil.
			—and subsequent Attacks on High Wood	...	20th–25th July	Road Flers — Longueval — Bazentin-le-Grand—Bazentin-le-Petit—Martinpuich.
	(iii.) BATTLE OF DELVILLE WOOD	...	...	...	15th July–3rd September	Delville Wood.
	(iv.) BATTLE OF POZIERES RIDGE	Fighting for Mouquet Farm	...	...	23rd July–3rd September	Road Bazentin-le-Petit — Contalmaison—Fricourt — Bécourt — Albert (exclusive) thence the river Ancre.

17

(v.) BATTLE OF GUILLEMONT	...	...	3rd–6th September	The Combles valley to Hardecourt: thence road to Maricourt—Montauban—Longueval.
(vi.) BATTLE OF GINCHY	...	...	9th September	
(vii.) BATTLE OF FLERS—COURCELETTE	Capture of Martinpuich	...	15th–22nd September	The Combles valley to Hardecourt: thence road to Maricourt—Fricourt—Bécourt—Albert (exclusive): thence the river Ancre.
(viii.) BATTLE OF MORVAL	Capture of Combles Capture of Lesbœufs Capture of Guendecourt	...	25th–28th September	The Combles valley to Hardecourt: thence road to Maricourt—Fricourt—Bécourt—la Boisselle—Bapaume.
(ix.) BATTLE OF THIEPVAL RIDGE	...	...	26th–28th September	The Bapaume road to Albert (exclusive): thence road to Martinsart—Englebelmer—Auchonvillers—Serre.
(x.) BATTLE OF THE TRANSLOY RIDGES	Capture of Eaucourt l'Abbaye Capture of le Sars Attacks on the Butte de Warlencourt	...	1st–18th October	The valley from Sailly-Saillisel to Combles: thence road to Ginchy—Longueval—Martinpuich—Courcelette: thence the valley to Warlencourt.
(xi.) BATTLE OF THE ANCRE HEIGHTS	Capture of Schwaben and Stuff Redoubts and Regina Trench	...	1st October – 11th November	Road Pys – le Sars – Martinpuich – Contalmaison – la Boisselle – Aveluy – Martinsart – Mesnil – Hamel.
(xii.) BATTLE OF THE ANCRE, 1916	Capture of Beaumont Hamel	...	13th–18th November	The Bapaume road to la Boisselle: thence road to Aveluy—Martinsart—Englebelmer—Mailly-Maillet—Colincamps—Hébuterne—Puisieux-au-Mont.

† On the Aubers Ridge.

FRANCE AND FLANDERS—continued.

OPERATIONS.	BATTLES.		ACTIONS, &c.	MISCELLANEOUS INCIDENTS.	LIMITS.	
	NAME.	TACTICAL INCIDENTS INCLUDED.			CHRONOLOGICAL.	GEOGRAPHICAL.

IV.—THE ADVANCE TO THE HINDENBURG LINE, 1917.

OPERATIONS.	NAME.	TACTICAL INCIDENTS INCLUDED.	ACTIONS, &c.	MISCELLANEOUS INCIDENTS.	CHRONOLOGICAL.	GEOGRAPHICAL.
Operations on the Ancre (11th January—13th March, 1917.)	...	...	Actions of Miraumont	...	17th and 18th February	Road Pys—Courcelette—Thiepval—Hamel—Beaucourt.
			Capture of the Thilloys	...	25th February–2nd March	Road Bapaume—Gueudecourt (exclusive)—le Sars—Pys (exclusive)—Grevillers.
			Capture of Irles	...	10th March	Road Warlencourt—Courcelette—Miraumont : thence the railway to Achiet-le-Grand.
German Retreat to the Hindenburg Line (14th March—5th April, 1917.)	...	...	Capture of Bapaume	...	17th March	*
			...	Occupation of Péronne	18th March	*

V.—THE ALLIED OFFENSIVES, 1917.

OPERATIONS.	NAME.	TACTICAL INCIDENTS INCLUDED.	ACTIONS, &c.	MISCELLANEOUS INCIDENTS.	CHRONOLOGICAL.	GEOGRAPHICAL.
The Arras Offensive (9th April–15th May, 1917.)	THE BATTLES OF ARRAS, 1917	...	...	...	9th April–4th May.	
	(i.) BATTLE OF VIMY RIDGE	...	...	...	} 9th–14th April	Willerval — Marœuil — Mont St. Eloy — Ablain-St. Nazaire—Liévin—Lens.
	FIRST BATTLE OF THE SCARPE, 1917	Capture of Monchy-le-Preux Capture of Wancourt Ridge	...	...		Chérisy—Hamelincourt — Marœuil (exclusive)—Willerval (exclusive).
	(ii.) SECOND BATTLE OF THE SCARPE, 1917	Capture of Guémappe Capture of Gavrelle	...	...	23rd–24th April	The river Sensée from Vis-en-Artois to Ervillers (exclusive) : thence a line to Dainville (exclusive)—Bailleul—Oppy.
			—with subsidiary Attack on la Coulotte	...	23rd April.	Road Méricourt— Vimy—Neuville-St. Vaast—la Targette—Souchez : thence the river Souchez.
	(iii.) BATTLE OF ARLEUX	...	...	...	28th–29th April	Boiry-Notre-Dame — Monchy-le-Preux — Beaurains — Roclincourt— Vimy—Acheville.
	(iv.) THIRD BATTLE OF THE SCARPE, 1917	Capture of Fresnoy	...	...	3rd–4th May	The river Sensée from Vis-en-Artois to St. Léger : thence a line to Boyelles—Beaurains—Roclincourt—Vimy—Acheville.

				Dates	Area
			—with subsequent (i.) Capture of Roeux	13th–14th May	Boiry-Notre-Dame — Monchy-le-Preux —Athies—Fresnes-lez-Montauban.
			(ii.) Capture of Oppy Wood	28th June	*
—with flanking operations (a.) round Bullecourt (11th April–16th June.)		BATTLE OF BULLECOURT	First Attack on Bullecourt	11th April	Road Quéant (exclusive)—Noreuil—Vaulx-Vraucourt—"l'Homme Mort"—Ecoust-St. Mein—Hendecourt.
			German Attack on Lagnicourt	15th April	The railway Havrincourt—Jeugny: thence road to Vaulx-Vraucourt—Ecoust-St. Mein—Hendecourt.
			...	3rd–17th May	Road Quéant (exclusive)—Noreuil—Vaulx-Vraucourt—"l'Homme Mort"—Ecoust-St. Mein—Hendecourt.
			Actions on the Hindenburg Line	20th May–16th June	Road Quéant (exclusive)—Noreuil—Vaulx-Vraucourt—"l'Homme Mort"—Ecoust-St. Mein—Hendecourt.
(b.) towards Lens... (3rd June–30th August.)		BATTLE OF HILL 70	Affairs south of the Souchez River	3rd–28th June	Road Méricourt—Vimy—Neuville-St. Vaast—la Targette—Souchez: thence the river Souchez.
			Capture of Avion	26th–29th June	Road Méricourt—Vimy—Neuville-St. Vaast—la Targette—Souchez: thence the river Souchez.
			...	15th–25th August	The river Souchez from Lens to Angres: thence a line to Grenay — Vermelles Station—Vendin-le-Vieil
The Flanders Offensive (7th June–10th November, 1917.)	THE BATTLE OF MESSINES, 1917	Capture of Wytschaete	...	7th–14th June	Road Frelinghien—le Bizet—Petit Pont — Neuve Eglise— Dranoutre—Locre — la Clytte — Dickebusch — Kruisstraat: thence a line to Zillebeke—Gheluvelt.
			German Attack on Nieuport	10th–11th July	Between the Nieuport Canal and the sea, east of the road from Wulpen to Oost-Dunkerke Bains.

FRANCE AND FLANDERS—continued.

V.—THE ALLIED OFFENSIVES. 1917—continued.

OPERATIONS.	BATTLES.		ACTIONS, &c.	MISCELLANEOUS INCIDENTS.	LIMITS.	
	NAME.	TACTICAL INCIDENTS INCLUDED.			CHRONOLOGICAL.	GEOGRAPHICAL.
The Flanders Offensive—continued.	THE BATTLES OF YPRES, 1917	...	...	...	31st July — 10th November.	
	(i.) BATTLE OF PILCKEM RIDGE	...	—with subsequent Capture of Westhoek	...	31st July — 2nd August	The Comines—Ypres Canal as far as Voormezeele; thence road to Vlamertinghe Château—Elverdinghe Château—Woesten—Bixschoote.
	(ii.) BATTLE OF LANGEMARCK, 1917	...	...	...	10th August	
	(iii.) BATTLE OF THE MENIN ROAD RIDGE	...	...	...	16th–18th August	
	(iv.) BATTLE OF POLYGON WOOD	...	...	...	20th–25th September	
	(v.) BATTLE OF BROODSEINDE	...	...	...	26th September–3rd October	
	(vi.) BATTLE OF POELCAPPELLE	...	...	...	4th October	
	(vii.) FIRST BATTLE OF PASSCHENDAELE	...	...	...	9th October	
	(viii.) SECOND BATTLE OF PASSCHENDAELE	...	...	...	12th October	
					26th October — 10th November	
The Cambrai Operations (20th November—7th December, 1917.)	BATTLE OF CAMBRAI, 1917	The Tank Attack	...	...	20th November–3rd December.	Road Honnecourt — Villers-Guislain — Gouzeaucourt — Metz — Ruyaulcourt — Beaumetz — Morchies — Lagnicourt — Quéant.
		Capture of Bourlon Wood	...	...	20th–21st November	
		The German Counter-Attacks	...	...	23rd–28th November	
			—with subsequent Action of Welch Ridge	...	30th November–3rd December	Road Bonssoy — Villers-Faucon — Fins — Ruyaulcourt and thence as above.
					30th December	Road Banteux—Gonnelieu—Gouzeaucourt Station; thence the railway to Marcoing.

VI.—THE GERMAN OFFENSIVES, 1918.

The Offensive in Picardy (21st March–5th April, 1918.)	THE FIRST BATTLES OF THE SOMME, 1918	‡	...	21st March – 5th April.
	(i.) BATTLE OF ST. QUENTIN	‡	...	21st–23rd March	The river Oise to Chauny; thence road to Guiscard—Ham—Péronne—Bapaume—Boyelles; thence the river Cojeul.
			Actions at the Somme Crossings	21st–23rd March	The line of the Somme from Ham to Hem.
	(ii.) FIRST BATTLE OF BAPAUME†	‡	...	24th–25th March	The river Somme to Bray; thence road to Albert — Martinsart — Sailly-au-Bois — Monchy-au-Bois — Arras; thence the river Scarpe.
	(iii.) BATTLE OF ROSIÈRES	‡	...	26th–27th March	Between the rivers Avre and Somme, east of road Pierrepont—Mézières—Demuin—Villers Bretonneux—Corbie.
	(iv.) FIRST BATTLE OF ARRAS, 1918	‡	...	28th March	Road Authuille — Bertrancourt — Couin—Gaudiempré—Arras—Oppy.
	(v.) BATTLE OF THE AVRE	‡	...	4th April	Between the rivers Avre and Somme.
	(vi.) BATTLE OF THE ANCRE, 1918	‡	...	5th April	Road Méricourt l'Abbé— Warloy—Acheux—Souastre—Monchy-au-Bois—Ayette.
			—with subsequent (i.) Actions of Villers Bretonneux	24th–25th April	Between the rivers Avre and Somme.
			(ii.) Capture of Hamel	4th July	Between the road Lamotte—Longueau and the Somme.
The Offensive in Flanders (9th–29th April, 1918.)	THE BATTLES OF THE LYS	...	...	9th–29th April.	
	(i.) BATTLE OF ESTAIRES	First Defence of Givenchy, 1918	...	9th–11th April	The la Bassée Canal to Béthune; thence road to St. Venant; thence a line to Vieux Berquin; from there the road to Bailleul—Armentières (all exclusive).
	(ii.) BATTLE OF MESSINES, 1918	Loss of Hill 63	...	10th–11th April	Road Armentières — Bailleul — Locre — Dickebusch — Voormezeele; thence the Ypres—Comines Canal.

† The name of "Bapaume" has been adopted for this battle in the German official list.
‡ Owing to the confused nature of the fighting over such a great area, the Committee consider that it is undesirable to attempt to mention tactical incidents.

FRANCE AND FLANDERS—continued.

OPERATIONS.	BATTLES.		ACTIONS, &c.	MISCELLANEOUS INCIDENTS.	LIMITS.	
	NAME.	TACTICAL INCIDENTS INCLUDED.			CHRONOLOGICAL.	GEOGRAPHICAL.

VI.—THE GERMAN OFFENSIVES, 1918—continued.

OPERATIONS.	NAME.	TACTICAL INCIDENTS INCLUDED.	ACTIONS, &c.	MISCELLANEOUS INCIDENTS.	CHRONOLOGICAL.	GEOGRAPHICAL.
The Offensive in Flanders ... (continued.)	THE BATTLES OF THE LYS—continued.					
	(iii.) BATTLE OF HAZEBROUCK	Defence of Hinges Ridge Defence of Nieppe Forest	...	...	12th–15th April	The river Lawe from le Cœsan to Béthune (exclusive): thence the railway by Hazebrouck (exclusive) to Caestre: thence road to Mont des Cats—Meteren.
	(iv.) BATTLE OF BAILLEUL	Defence of Neuve Eglise	...	...	13th–15th April	Road Meteren—Mont des Cats—Boeschepe—Reninghelst—Ouderdom—Vierstraat—Wytschaete.
	(v.) FIRST BATTLE OF KEMMEL RIDGE	...	...	...	17th–19th April	Road Meteren—Mont des Cats—Boeschepe—Reninghelst—Ouderdom—Vierstraat—Wytschaete.
	(vi.) BATTLE OF BÉTHUNE	Second Defence of Givenchy, 1918	...	...	18th April	The la Bassée Canal to Béthune (exclusive): thence road to Chocques—Busnes—St. Venant—Merville.
	(vii.) SECOND BATTLE OF KEMMEL RIDGE	...	...	...	25th–26th April	Road Meteren—Mont des Cats—Boeschepe—Reninghelst—Vlamertinghe—Ypres (exclusive): thence the Comines Canal.
	(viii.) BATTLE OF THE SCHERPENBERG	...	...	...	29th April	Road St. Jans Cappel—Boeschepe—Reninghelst—Vlamertinghe—Ypres (exclusive): thence the Comines Canal.
			—with subsequent (i.) Action of la Becque	...	28th June	The Lys Canal to St. Venant (exclusive): thence the road to Morbecque: thence a line to Swartenbrouck—Vieux Berquin.
			(ii.) Capture of Meteren	...	19th July	The Meteren Becque to Flêtre: thence a line to Fontaine Houck—Bailleul Station.
The Offensive in Champagne (27th May–6th June, 1918.)	BATTLE OF THE AISNE, 1918†	‡	...	...	27th May–6th June	Between the Chemin des Dames and the Montagne de Reims, east of the line Bouconville—Fismes—Verneuil.

VII.—THE ADVANCE TO VICTORY, 1918.

The Counter-Attack in Champagne (20th July—2nd August, 1918.)	THE BATTLES OF THE MARNE, 1918†	...	...	20th July - 2nd August.	
	(i.) BATTLE OF THE SOISSONNAIS AND OF THE OURCQ‡	Attack on Buzancy (28th July.) Capture of the Beugneux Ridge	...	23rd July - 2nd August	Between the rivers Ourcq and Aisne, east of the line Breny—Vierzy—Pommiers.
	(ii.) BATTLE OF TARDENOIS	The fighting for the Ardre Valley	...	20th–31st July	The Valley of the Ardre above Sarcy.
The Advance in Picardy (8th August–3rd September, 1918.)	THE BATTLE OF AMIENS	...	—with subsequent Actions round Damery	8th–11th August	Between the roads Amiens—Roye and Amiens—Albert (Amiens exclusive).
				15th–17th August	Road Roye—Bouchoir—Rosières: thence the railway to Puzeaux.
The Advance in Flanders (18th August–6th September, 1918)	...	...	Action of Outtersteene Ridge	18th August	The railway from Bailleul to Strazeele Station: thence road to Strazeele—Meteren.
The Advance in Picardy (continued) (21st August–3rd September)	THE SECOND BATTLES OF THE SOMME, 1918	...	...	21st August - 3rd September.	
	(i.) BATTLE OF ALBERT, 1918	Capture of Chuignes	...	21st–23rd August	Road Chaulnes — Lamotte — Corbie — Warloy—Acheux—Souastre—Berles-au-Bois—Brétencourt—Hénineli.
	(ii.) SECOND BATTLE OF BAPAUME	Capture of Mont St. Quentin	...	31st August - 3rd September	Road Athies—Chaulnes—Rosières—Bray—Miraumont — Hamelincourt — St. Léger: thence a line to Noreuil—Mœuvres.
			Occupation of Péronne	1st September	*

† The French names for these battles have been adopted, but the tactical incidents and limits refer only to the operations of the British troops which formed part of the French Armies.
‡ Owing to the confused nature of the fighting over such a great area, the Committee consider that it is undesirable to attempt to mention tactical incidents.

FRANCE AND FLANDERS—continued.

VII.—THE ADVANCE TO VICTORY, 1918—continued.

OPERATIONS.	BATTLES.		ACTIONS, &c.	MISCELLANEOUS INCIDENTS.	LIMITS.	
	NAME.	TACTICAL INCIDENTS INCLUDED.			CHRONOLOGICAL.	GEOGRAPHICAL.
The Breaking of the Hindenburg Line (26th August–12th October, 1918)	THE SECOND BATTLES OF ARRAS, 1918	...	...	...	26th August – 3rd September.	
	(i.) BATTLE OF THE SCARPE, 1918	Capture of Monchy-le-Preux	...	...	26th–30th August	Noreuil (exclusive)—St. Léger (exclusive)—Boisleux-au-Mont—Roclincourt—Bailleul—Oppy.
	(ii.) BATTLE OF THE DROCOURT–QUÉANT LINE	...	...	...	2nd–3rd September	Mœuvres (exclusive)—Noreuil (exclusive)—St. Léger (exclusive)—Monchy-le-Preux—Pelves: thence the river Scarpe.
	THE BATTLES OF THE HINDENBURG LINE				12th September–9th October.	
	(i.) BATTLE OF HAVRINCOURT	...	...	...	12th September	Road Gouzeaucourt — Fins — Ytres — Beaumetz—Morchies: thence a line to Mœuvres.
	(ii.) BATTLE OF ÉPÉHY	...	...	...	18th September	St. Quentin (exclusive) — Beauvois — Cartigny — Manancourt: thence by the southern edge of Havrincourt Wood to Villers Plouich.
	(iii.) BATTLE OF THE CANAL DU NORD	Capture of Bourlon Wood	...	...	27th September–1st October	Road Bantueux—Gouzeaucourt (exclusive)—Fins (exclusive)—Ytres — Lagnicourt—Vis-en-Artois: thence the river Sensée.
	(iv.) BATTLE OF THE ST. QUENTIN CANAL	Passage at Bellenglise. Capture of Bellicourt Tunnel Defences	...	...	29th September–2nd October	Road St. Quentin (exclusive) – Vermand—Roisel — Villers-Faucon — Fins — Gouzeaucourt—Banteux (exclusive).
	(v.) BATTLE OF THE BEAUREVOIR LINE	...	...	...	3rd–5th October	Road Sequehart — Bellenglise — Pontru — Épehy—Vendhuille—Villers-Outréaux.
	(vi.) BATTLE OF CAMBRAI, 1918	Capture of Villers-Outréaux Capture of Cambrai	...	...	8th–9th October	Road Fresnoy—Sequehart— Bellenglise—Bellicourt — Vendhuille — Villers-Guislain — Villers-Plouich — Graincourt—Bourlon—Oisy-le-Verger: thence the river Sensée.
—including The Pursuit to the Selle (9th–12th October)	...	...	...	...	9th–12th October.	

24

The Final Advance:—

† *Flanders* (28th September—11th November)	BATTLE OF YPRES, 1918	...	...	28th September–2nd October	Road Armentières — Bailleul — Locre — Reninghelst — Vlamertinghe Château — Elverdinghe Château: thence a line to Mooralede.
	BATTLE OF COURTRAI	*with subsequent* (i.) Action of Ooteghem	...	14th–19th October	Dottignies — Comine — Messines: thence along the ridge to Passchendaele: thence a line to Mooralede—Lendelete.
			...	25th October	Road Bossuyt—St. Genois—Sweveghem—Nieuwe Kappaart: thence the stream to Waereghem, and from there the road to Wortegem.
		(ii.) Action of Tieghem	...	31st October	The river Escaut to Avelghem; thence road to Heestert—Kattestraat—Vichte—Heirweg—Mooregem—Wortegem.
† *Artois* (2nd October—11th November)	...	...	Capture of Douai	17th October	*
† *Picardy* (17th October—11th November)	BATTLE OF THE SELLE	...	...	17th–25th October	The railway Boué — Itusigny — Caudry: thence the stream to its junction with the river Escaut: thence the latter.
	BATTLE OF VALENCIENNES	Capture of Mont Houy	...	1st–2nd November	The Bavai—Cambrai road as far as Vendegies: thence the stream to its junction with the river Escaut: thence a line to Wallers: thence along the southern edge of the forests of Vicoigne and Raismes.
	BATTLE OF THE SAMBRE	Passage of the Sambre—Oise Canal Capture of le Quesnoy	*with subsequent* (i.) Passage of the Grande Honnelle *and*	4th November	The railway Boué — le Cateau (*exclusive*): thence road to Bonneries — Fumars — Onnaing: thence the railway to Mons.
			(ii.) Capture of Mons	5th–7th November	Between the Bavai—Cambrai road and the Valenciennes—Mons railway, east of the line Warguies—Onnaing.
				11th November	*

† Compare Chaucer:—

"With him ther was his sonne, a yong Squyer
....
"Of twenty yeer he was of age, I gesse,
"And he had been some tyme in chivalrye
"In Flaundres, in Artoys, and in Picardie."

ITALY.

OPERATIONS.	BATTLES.		ACTIONS, &c.	MISCELLANEOUS INCIDENTS.	LIMITS.†	
	NAME.†	TACTICAL INCIDENTS INCLUDED.†			CHRONOLOGICAL.	GEOGRAPHICAL.
The Italian Offensive, 1917	TENTH BATTLE OF THE ISONZO	...	...	...	12th May–8th June	Between Gorizia and the sea, east of the Isonzo.
	ELEVENTH BATTLE OF THE ISONZO	...	...	...	17th August–19th September	Between Gorizia and the sea, east of the Isonzo.
The Austrian Offensive, 1917 —*including The Retreat to the Piave.*	TWELFTH BATTLE OF THE ISONZO	The stand on the Carso	...	...	24th October–18th November	Between the Carso and the Piave.
The Austrian Offensive, 1918	THE BATTLE OF THE PIAVE	...	...	...	15th–24th June	From the Astico to the Sea.
		The fighting on the Asiago Plateau	...	...	15th–16th June	The Asiago Plateau, north of the line Conco—Cogollo.
The Italian Offensive, 1918	THE BATTLE OF VITTORIO VENETO	...	...	...	24th October–4th November	
		Passage of the Piave	...	...	23rd October–4th November	Between the railways Treviso—Conegliano and Treviso—Oderzo.
		The fighting in the Val d'Assa	...	...	1st–4th November	The Val d'Assa, north of Asiago.

† The Italian names for these battles have been adopted, but the tactical incidents and limits refer only to the operations of the British troops which formed part of the Italian Armies. In 1917 these consisted of brigades of heavy artillery; in 1918 of complete British formations.

MACEDONIA.

Retreat from Serbia on Salonika (December, 1915.)	...	...	Actions of Kosturino	...	7th–8th December	North of the Serbo-Greek frontier.
Doiran Operations, 1916 (August–September.)	...	...	Affairs of Horseshoe Hill	...	10th–18th August	Between the Göl Ayak and the Selimli Dere.
			Action of Machukovo	...	13th–14th September	Between the Selimli Dere and the river Vardar.
Operations in the Struma Valley (1916–1918.)	...	...	Action of the Karajaköi's including Capture of Yenıköi	...	30th September–4th October, 1916	The Struma Valley above Lake Takhinos.
			Affair of Barakli Juma's	...	31st October, 1916	
1917 Offensive (April–May.)	...	BATTLE OF DOIRAN, 1917†	...	...	24th–25th April and 8th–9th May	Between the Doiran—Karasuli railway and the river Vardar
1918 Offensive (1st–30th September.)	...	...	Capture of the Roche Noir Salient	...	1st–2nd September	Between the Vardar and the line Mayadag —Pardovitza.
		BATTLE OF DOIRAN, 1918 ‡	...	...	1sth–10th September	Between the Dova Tepe—Doiran—Karasuli railway and the river Vardar.
—including The Pursuit to the Strumitsa Valley (22nd–30th September.)	...	...	...	...	22nd–30th September	Dova Tepe—Doiran—Karasuli: thence the river Vardar to the confluence of the Koja Dere: thence the latter

† This battle forms part of the "Battle of the Vardar." *(French official title.)*
‡ This battle forms part of the "Battle of Monastir—Doiran." *(French official title.)*

DARDANELLES.

OPERATIONS.	BATTLES.		ACTIONS, &c.	MISCELLANEOUS INCIDENTS.	LIMITS.	
	NAME.	TACTICAL INCIDENTS INCLUDED.			CHRONOLOGICAL.	GEOGRAPHICAL.
Helles Operations (25th April, 1915–8th January, 1916.)	THE BATTLES OF HELLES	...	...	...	25th April–8th June.	
	(i.) THE LANDING AT CAPE HELLES	Capture of Sedd el Bahr	—with subsidiary Landing at Kum Kale	...	25th–28th April	All landings on the southern end of the Gallipoli Peninsula. Landing by French force on the Asiatic shore.
	(ii.) FIRST BATTLE OF KRITHIA	...	Actions of Eski Hissarlik†	...	28th April	From the Straits on the right to the sea on the left.
	(iii.) SECOND BATTLE OF KRITHIA	First Action of Kereves Dere†	...	...	1st–2nd May 6th–8th May	
	(iv.) THIRD BATTLE OF KRITHIA	Second Action of Kereves Dere†	Affair of Gurkha Bluff	...	4th June	From Gully Ravine on the right to the sea on the left. From the Straits on the right to the sea on the left.
			Third Action of Kereves Dere†	...	21st June	From the Straits on the right to Achi Baba Nullah on the left.
			Action of Gully Ravine	...	28th June–2nd July	From East Krithia Nullah (*exclusive*) on the right to Achi Baba Nullah on the left.
			Fourth Action of Kereves Dere†	...	30th June	From the Straits on the right to Achi Baba Nullah on the left.
			Action of Achi Baba Nullah‡	...	12th–13th July	From the Straits on the right to the Sedd el Bahr–Krithia road on the left.
			Actions of Krithia Vineyard‡§	...	6th–13th August	From Achi Baba Nullah on the right to Gully Ravine (*exclusive*) on the left.
			Affair of the Krithia Nullahs	...	29th December	From the Achi Baba Nullah on the right to West Krithia Nullah on the left.
—including The Evacuation of Helles (7th–8th January, 1916.)	...	...	The last Turkish Attacks	...	7th January	From the Achi Baba Nullah on the right to the sea on the left.

29

Anzac and Suvla Operations (25th April–20th December, 1915.)	THE BATTLES OF ANZAC			25th April–30th June.	
	(i.) THE LANDING AT ANZAC			{ 25th–26th April	From Gabe Tepe (exclusive) to Fisherman's Hut (exclusive).
			—with subsidiary Demonstration in the Gulf of Xeros		
		Attack on The Chessboard		2nd May	*
		Affair of Quinn's Post		10th May	*
	(ii.) THE DEFENCE OF ANZAC			19th–21st May	From Gabe Tepe (exclusive) to Fisherman's Hut (exclusive).
		Affair of Holly Ridge		28th June	*
		Defence of Walker's Ridge		30th June	*
	THE BATTLES OF SUVLA			6th–21st August.	
	(i.) BATTLE OF SARI BAIR	Capture of Lone Pine Attack at Russell's Top		6th–10th August	South of the Azmak Dere.
	(ii.) THE LANDING AT SUVLA	Capture of Karakol Dagh Capture of Chocolate Hill		6th–15th August	North of the Azmak Dere.
			—with subsidiary Demonstration in the Gulf of Xeros	6th–7th August	*
	(iii.) BATTLE OF SCIMITAR HILL	Attack on "W" Hill		21st August	North of the Azmak Dere.
			—with subsidiary Actions of Hill 60 (Anzac)	21st and 27th August	Between the Azmak Dere and the Aghil Dere.
—including The Evacuation of Suvla and Anzac (19th–20th December, 1915.)				19th–20th December.	

† French official titles. ‡ The French titles for these actions are Fifth and Sixth Actions of Kereves Dere. § Subsidiary to the Battles of Suvla. ‖ Subsidiary to the Action of Gully Ravine.

EGYPT AND PALESTINE.

OPERATIONS.	BATTLES.		ACTIONS, &c.	MISCELLANEOUS INCIDENTS.	LIMITS.	
	NAME.	TACTICAL INCIDENTS INCLUDED.			CHRONOLOGICAL.	GEOGRAPHICAL.

SUDAN.

OPERATIONS.	NAME.	TACTICAL INCIDENTS INCLUDED.	ACTIONS, &c.	MISCELLANEOUS INCIDENTS.	CHRONOLOGICAL.	GEOGRAPHICAL.
Operations against the Sultan of Darfur (1st March–31st December, 1916.)	...	...	Affair of Beringiya	—with subsequent Occupation of El Fasher	22nd May 23rd May	* *
			Affair of Gyuba	...	6th November	*

WESTERN FRONTIER.

OPERATIONS.	NAME.	TACTICAL INCIDENTS INCLUDED.	ACTIONS, &c.	MISCELLANEOUS INCIDENTS.	CHRONOLOGICAL.	GEOGRAPHICAL.
Operations against the Senussi (23rd November, 1915–8th February 1917.)	...	...	Affair of the Wadi Senab	...	11th–13th December, 1915	Area covered by the force under Lieut.-Colonel J. L. R. Gordon.
			Affair of the Wadi Majid	...	25th December, 1915	Area covered by the two columns under Major-General A. Wallace.
			Affair of Halazin	...	23rd January, 1916	
			Action of Agagiya	...	26th February, 1916	Area covered by the force under Brigadier-General H. T. Lukin.
			Affairs in the Dakhla Oasis	...	17th–22nd October, 1916	*
			Affairs near the Siwa Oasis	...	3rd–5th February, 1917	Siwa Oasis to Munasib.

EASTERN FRONTIER AND PALESTINE.

I.—The Defence of Egypt.

Defence of the Suez Canal... (26th January, 1915–12th August, 1916)	...	...	Actions on the Suez Canal	...	3rd–4th February, 1915	East of the Suez–Qantara Railway.
			Affair of Qatia	...	23rd April, 1916	East of the Canal and north of El Ferdan Station.
	BATTLE OF RUMANI		...	...	4th–5th August, 1916	East of the Canal and north of Ismailia.
Operations in the Sinai Peninsula... (15th November, 1916–9th January, 1917.)	...		Affair of Magdhaba	...	23rd December, 1916	South and east of Bir Lahfan.
	...		Action of Rafah	...	9th January, 1917	North and east of Sheikh Zow'id.

31

32

EGYPT AND PALESTINE—continued.

II.—The Invasion of Palestine.

OPERATIONS.	BATTLES.		ACTIONS, &c.	MISCELLANEOUS INCIDENTS.	LIMITS.	
	NAME.	TACTICAL INCIDENTS INCLUDED.			CHRONOLOGICAL.	GEOGRAPHICAL.
The First Offensive ... (24th March–19th April, 1917.)	FIRST BATTLE OF GAZA	...	...	...	26th–27th March	} North of the line Beersheba—Rein'.
	SECOND BATTLE OF GAZA	...	...	...	17th–19th April	
The Second Offensive (27th October – 16th November, 1917.)	THIRD BATTLE OF GAZA	Capture of Beersheba. Capture of the Sheria Position	...	...	27th October – 7th November	North of the Wadi Ghuzze.
			Affair of Huj	...	8th November	} North of the line Beersheba—Gaza and west of the Beersheba—Jerusalem road.
			Action of El Mughar	...	13th November	
				—with subsequent Occupation of Junction Station	14th November	
Jerusalem Operations (17th November–30th December, 1917.)	BATTLE OF NEBI SAMWIL	...	...	...	17th–24th November	} North and east of the line Hebron—Junction Station.
	DEFENCE OF JERUSALEM	...	Capture of Jerusalem	...	7th–9th December	
		...	...	...	26th–30th December	
	—with subsidiary BATTLE OF JAFFA	...	...	...	21st–22nd December	Between the Tul Keram—Junction Station—Jaffa railway and the sea.

Operations in and beyond the Jordan Valley. (19th February–4th May, 1918.)	...	Capture of Jericho	...	19th–21st February	Between the Bethlehem—Nablus road and the Jordan, north of the line Jerusalem—Dead Sea.
		Passage of the Jordan	...	21st–23rd March	} East of the Jordan.
		First Action of Es Salt	...	24th–25th March	
		First Attack on Amman	...	27th–30th March	
		Turkish Attack on the Jordan Bridgeheads	...	11th April	
		Second Action of Es Salt	...	30th April–4th May	
—with subsidiary Arab Operations in the Mountains of Moab. (March and April, 1918.)	...	...	...	March and April	
Local Operations. 1918	...	Actions of Tel Asur	...	8th–12th March	West of the Jordan, and north of the line Jericho—Ram Allah—Jaffa.
	...	Affair of Abu Telul	...	14th July	*
The Final Offensive... (18th September–31st October, 1918.)	THE BATTLES OF MEGIDDO	...	...	18th–25th September.	
	(i.) BATTLE OF SHARON	...	...	} 19th–25th September	
	(ii.) BATTLE OF NABLUS	...	...		
		Actions beyond Jordan	...	23rd–30th September	Between the Hejaz Railway and the sea, north of the line Dhaba Station—mouth of Jordan—Arsuf.
		Capture of Amman	...	25th September	
		Capture of Dera'a†	...	27th September	
—including The Pursuit through Syria (26th September–31st October.)	...	Capture of Damascus	...	1st October	
		Affair of Haritan	...	26th October	North of the Haifa—Dera's railway.
			—with subsequent Occupation of Aleppo	26th October	

† Arab forces.

ARABIA.

HEJAZ.

OPERATIONS.	BATTLES.		ACTIONS, &c.	MISCELLANEOUS INCIDENTS.	LIMITS.	
	NAME.	TACTICAL INCIDENTS INCLUDED.			CHRONOLOGICAL.	GEOGRAPHICAL.
The Arab Revolt ... (June–December, 1916.)	...	...	Attack on Medina	...	6th June	*
			Capture of Jidda	...	9th June	*
			Capture of Mecca	...	10th June	*
			Capture of Yenbo	...	27th July	
			Capture of Taif	...	22nd September	*
Operations against the Hejaz Railway (October, 1916–November, 1918.)	...	...	...	...	October, 1916–November, 1918	From Ma'an to Medina.
Wejh Operations (January, 1917.)	...	...	Capture of Wejh	...	24th January	North of Yenbo.
Aqaba Operations (6th May–21st October, 1917.)	...	...	Affair of Aba e' Lissan	...	3rd July	*
				Occupation of Aqaba	6th July	*
			Turkish Attack on Petra	...	21st October	Between the Hejaz Railway and the Wadi 'Araba.

Tafile Operations (January–March, 1918.)	...	Actions for Et Tafile	1st–28th January	Between the Hejaz Railway and the Wadi Araba.
			27th January	El Mezra'a.
		Seizure of the Turkish Dead Sea Flotilla		
Ma'an Operations (April–September, 1918.)	...	Affair of Shahim Station	20th April	*
		Affair of Mudawara Station	6th August	*
		Evacuation of Ma'an	23rd September	*

Note.—The operations of the Arab forces which co-operated with the British Army in their operations beyond Jordan and in the final offensive in Syria have been included under EGYPT AND PALESTINE.

SOUTHERN ARABIA.

Operations in the Bab el Mandeb (1914–15.)	...	Capture of Sheikh Sa'id	10th November, 1914	Sheikh Sa'id Peninsula.
		Turkish Attack on Perim	14th–16th June, 1915	Perim Island (*Troops under the command of Captain H. A. C. Hutchinson*).
Defence of Aden (3rd July, 1915—31st October, 1918.)	...	Action of Lahej	4th–5th July, 1915	*
		Affair of Sheikh 'Othman	20th July, 1915	*
		Affair of Jabir	7th December, 1916	*
		Affair of Imad	22nd October, 1918	*

MESOPOTAMIA.

I.—THE CAMPAIGN IN LOWER MESOPOTAMIA.

OPERATIONS.	BATTLES.		ACTIONS &c.	MISCELLANEOUS INCIDENTS.	LIMITS.	
	NAME.	TACTICAL INCIDENTS INCLUDED.			CHRONOLOGICAL.	GEOGRAPHICAL.
Basra Operations (6th November, 1914–14th April, 1915.)	...	...	...	Landing at Fao	6th November	⎱ Delta of the Shatt al 'Arab up to Basra.
			Affair of Saihan	...	15th November	
			Affair of Sahil	...	17th November	
				—*with subsequent Occupation of Basra.*	22nd November	*
			First Action of Qurna	...	4th–8th December	The Tigris above Basra.
			Affair of Ahwaz	...	3rd March	North-west of Ahwaz (*exclusive*).
			Affair of Shaiba	...	3rd March	West of Shaiba (*exclusive*).
	BATTLE OF SHAIBA	...	...	...	12th–14th April	The inundation west of Basra and to the west of it.
Advance up the Tigris, 1915 (31st May–5th October.)	...	...	Second Action of Qurna	...	31st May	The Tigris above Qurna.
				—*with subsequent Occupation of Amara.*	3rd June	*
—*with subsidiary Operations on the Karkha River (7th May—3rd June.)*	BATTLE OF KUT, 1915	...	...	...	28th September	The Tigris above Sanna-i-Yat.
	...	...	Affair of Khafajiya	...	14th–16th May	*
Advance up the Euphrates, 1915 (27th June–25th July.)	...	...	Actions for Nasiriya	...	5th, 13th–14th, and 24th July.	The Euphrates west of Khor al Hammar.

86

II.—THE FIRST CAMPAIGN FOR BAGHDAD.

Advance on Baghdad, 1915 (11th November–6th December, 1915.)	BATTLE OF CTESIPHON —*with subsequent* DEFENCE OF KUT	...	...	22nd–24th November. 1st December	The Tigris above Lajj. The Tigris above Kut.
		The Christmas Eve Attack	Affair of Umm at Tubul	7th December, 1915–28th April, 1916.	
Attempts to relieve Kut (4th January–24th April, 1916.)	...	...	...	4th January–24th April.	
First Attempt (4th–23rd January.)	...	...	Action of Shaikh Sa'ad Action of the Wadi First Attack on Hanna	6th–8th January 13th–14th January 21st January	The Tigris above 'Ali Gharbi. The Tigris above Shaikh Sa'ad. The Tigris above the Wadi.
Second Attempt (7th–10th March.)	...	...	Attack on the Dujaila Redoubt	8th March	The Tigris above the Wadi
Third Attempt (1st–24th April.)	...	...	Action of Falahiya, —*including* *Capture of Hanna* First Attack on Sanna-i-Yat Second Attack on Sanna-i-Yat Action of Bait Aissa Third Attack on Sanna-i-Yat	5th April 6th April 9th April 17th–18th April 22nd April	The Tigris above the Wadi.
			Capitulation of Kut	29th April	
Euphrates Operations, 1916 (January–September.)	...	...	Affair of Butaniya Action of As Sahilan	14th January 11th September	North of Nasiriya

MESOPOTAMIA—continued.

III.—THE CAPTURE AND CONSOLIDATION OF BAGHDAD.

OPERATIONS.	BATTLES.		ACTIONS, &c.	MISCELLANEOUS INCIDENTS.	LIMITS.	
	NAME.	TACTICAL INCIDENTS INCLUDED.			CHRONOLOGICAL.	GEOGRAPHICAL.
Operations for the Capture of Kut, 1917 (13th December, 1916 – 25th February, 1917.)	BATTLES OF KUT, 1917		...	...	9th January – 24th February	The Tigris above Shaikh Sa'ad.
		Capture of the Khadairi Bend	...	...	9th–19th January	
		Capture of the Hai Salient	...	...	25th January – 5th February	
		Capture of the Dahra Bend	...	...	9th–16th February	
		Capture of Sanna-i-Yat	...	...	17th–24th February	
		Passage at the Shumran Bend	...	...	23rd–24th February	
—*with subsequent Pursuit to Baghdad* (*25th February–10th March, 1917.*)	...	...	Passage of the Diyala	...	7th–10th March	The Tigris above Kut.
				—*with subsequent Occupation of Baghdad*	11th March	*
Operations for the consolidation of the position at Baghdad (14th March–30th April, 1917.)	...	...	Action of Mushaidiya	...	14th March	The Tigris above Kadhimain.
			First Action of the Jabal Hamrin	...	25th March	Near Shahraban.
			Affair of Dali 'Abbas	...	27th–28th March	Right bank of the River Diyala above Ba'quba.
			Affair of Dogame	...	29th March	The Tigris above Mushaidiya.
			Affairs on the Nahr Khalis	...	9th–15th April	The Nahr Khalis Canal above Deltawa.
			Passage of the 'Adhaim	...	18th April	The Tigris above Dogame.
			Action of Istabulat	—*with subsequent Occupation of Samarra*	21st–22nd April	The Tigris above the Shatt al 'Adhaim.
					23rd–24th April	*
			Affairs on the Shatt al 'Adhaim	...	30th April	The Shatt al 'Adhaim above its junction with the Tigris.

IV.—THE CAMPAIGN IN UPPER MESOPOTAMIA.

Euphrates Operations, 1917-18 (8th July-13th April.)	...	...	Attack on Ramadi	...	11th-14th July	The Euphrates above Dhibban.
			Capture of Ramadi	...	28th-29th September	
			Action of Khan Baghdadi	—*with subsequent Occupation of Ana*	26th-27th March 28th March	The Euphrates above Hit. *
				Blockade of Najaf	1st-13th April	*
Tigris Operations, 1917 (1st October-6th December.)	...	...	Second Action of the Jabal Hamrin	...	18th-20th October	North of Shahraban.
			Actions for Tikrit	...	24th October, 2nd and 5th November	The Tigris above Al Ajik.
			Third Action of the Jabal Hamrin	...	3rd-6th December	North of Shahraban.
Kirkuk Operations (26th April-24th May, 1918.)	...	...	Action of Tuz Khurmatli	...	29th April	North of Kifri.
			Action of Fatha Gorge	...	23rd-24th October	The Tigris above Tikrit.
Advance on Mosul (23rd October-5th November, 1918.)	...	...	Actions on the Lesser Zab	...	25th October	The Tigris above Fatha Gorge.
	BATTLE OF SHARQAT		...	...	28th-30th October	
			Affair of Qaiyara	—*with subsequent Occupation of Mosul*	30th October 3rd November	*

PERSIA AND CENTRAL ASIA.

SOUTH PERSIA AND THE PERSIAN GULF.

OPERATIONS.	BATTLES.		ACTIONS, &c.	MISCELLANEOUS INCIDENTS.	LIMITS.	
	NAME.	TACTICAL INCIDENTS INCLUDED.			CHRONOLOGICAL.	GEOGRAPHICAL.
Defence of the Gulf Ports, 1915	...	...	Defence of Muscat	...	10th–11th January	*
			Defence of Jask	...	16th–17th April	*
			Defence of Chahbar	...	2nd–3rd May	*
			Destruction of Dilbar	...	12th–16th August	*
			Defence of Bushire	...	9th September	*
—with subsequent Operations of the Makran Mission (11th April, 1916–2nd February, 1917.)	...	...	...	...	...	Persian Makran.
Establishment of order, 1916	...	...	Capture of Saidabad	...	28th September	*
			...	Occupation of Shiraz and formation of the South Persia Rifles	12th November	Fars.
			Affair of Dasht-i-Arjan	...	25th December	*
Opening of the trade routes (1st January–30th November, 1917.)	...	...	Affair of Kafta	...	5th July	*
			Affairs in the Leshani country	...	19th–30th September	The valley on the north side of Lake Niriz
			Affairs in the Chahar Rah country	...	1st–21st October	Northern Fars.

Recrudescence of disorders (14th December, 1917-31st January, 1918.)	...	...	...	Affairs of Gumun	...	24th-27th January	Arsinjan district, east of the Shiraz—Deh Bid road.
Operations in Northern Fars (3rd-23rd May, 1918.)	...	...	...	Affair of Ziarat	...	13th-14th May	*
Qashqa Operations, 1918 ...	...	...	...	Affair of Kuh-i-Khan	...	16th May	*
				Action of Deh Shaikh	...	25th-26th May	*
					Persian Mutiny at Khan-i-Zinian	25th May	*
				Action of Ahmadabad	...	16th June	*
				Affair of Chanar Rahdar	...	7th-8th July	*
				Defence and Relief of Abadeh	Persian Mutiny	28th June-17th July	*
				Defence and Relief of Firuzabad	...	16th-24th October	Firuzabad and the Khajai valley.
Persian Operations round Isfahan and in Fars, 1919	...	...	...	Capture of Kadarjan	...	10th June	*
				Capture of Feragheh	...	8th August	*
Establishment of line of communication between Bushire and Shiraz (29th September, 1918-10th March, 1919.)					Consolidation of the coastal belt and occupation of Borazjun	29th September-23rd October	Between Bushire and Borazjun.
				Affair of Lardeh	...	31st October	*
					Seizure of the Kamarij Pass	20th December	*
					Occupation of Kazarun	27th January	*
					Junction between the Bushire and Shiraz Columns	28th January	Main Kotal
					Punitive measures in Southern Fars	11th December-10th March	Area Bushire—Kazarun—Shiraz—Firuzabad.

PERSIA AND CENTRAL ASIA—continued.

EAST PERSIA AND TRANS-CASPIA.

OPERATIONS.	BATTLES.		ACTIONS, &c.	MISCELLANEOUS INCIDENTS.	CHRONOLOGICAL.	LIMITS.	
	NAME.	TACTICAL INCIDENTS INCLUDED.				CHRONOLOGICAL.	GEOGRAPHICAL.
Establishment of the East Persia Cordon (29th July, 1915–31st January, 1918.)	...	...	...	Occupation of Birjand and junction with Russian Cordon	7th October, 1915	The Nushki—Kacha—Birjand road.	
				Captures of German agents	17th January and 8th August, 1916	Deh Salm and Sehdeh.	
			Affair of Lirudik	...	13th–14th April, 1916	*	
			Affair of Kundi	...	17th–18th April, 1916	*	
			Affair of the Gusht Defile	Occupation of Kwash (Vasht)	11th May, 1916	*	
			...	...	19th–21st July, 1916	*	
			Affair of Kalmas	...	28th September, 1916	*	
Extension of the Cordon into Khorasan (1st February–18th July, 1918.)	...	...	...	Occupation of Meshed	3rd March	*	

Operations in Trans-Caspia against the Bolsheviks (19th July, 1918–15th March, 1919.)	...	Affairs near Kaakhka	...	28th August, 11th and 18th September
		Action of Dushak	...	12th October
			—*with subsequent* Occupation of Merv	1st November
		Action of Annenkovo	...	16th January

NORTH-WEST PERSIA AND THE CASPIAN, 1918.

Establishment of line of communication between Baghdad and the Caspian (27th January–28th July.)	...	Affair near Zuhab	...	25th April
		Defence of Resht	...	20th July
Caspian Operations ... (August–September.)	...	...	Occupation of Baku	4th August
			Occupation of Krasnovodsk	27th August
		Defence of Baku	...	26th August–15th September.
Azerbaijan Operations ... (September.)	...	Rearguard Actions from Mianeh	...	5th–14th September
				North-west of Nikpai.

INDIA.[†]

NORTH-WEST FRONTIER AND BALUCHISTAN, 1914–1918.

North-West Frontier.

OPERATIONS.	BATTLES.		ACTIONS, &c.	MISCELLANEOUS INCIDENTS.	LIMITS.	
	NAME.	TACTICAL INCIDENTS INCLUDED.			CHRONOLOGICAL.	GEOGRAPHICAL.
Operations in the Tochi (28th November, 1914–27th March, 1915.)	...	...	Affair of Miran Shah	...	28th–29th November	*
			Affair of Spina Khaisora	...	7th January	*
			Action of Dardoni	...	25th–26th March	*
Operations against the Mohmands (14th–19th April, 1915.)	...	...	First Affair of Hafiz Kor	...	18th April	North-west of road Abazai—Shabkadr—Michni.
Operations against the Mohmands, Bunerwals and Swatis (17th August–28th October, 1915.)	...	...	Affair near Rustam	...	17th August	*
			Affair of Surkiawi	...	26th August	*
			Affairs of Landakai and Kak Fort	...	27th–29th August	Swat Valley above Thana.
			Affairs near Malandri	...	28th–31st August	*
			Action of Hafiz Kor	...	5th September	North-west of road Abazai—Shabkadr—Michni.
			Second Affair of Hafiz Kor	...	9th October	North-west of road Abazai—Shabkadr—Michni.
			Affair near Wuch	...	27th October	Wuch Valley north of Chakdarra (exclusive).

The Mohmand Blockade (30th September, 1916–18th July, 1917.)	...	Third Affair of Hafiz Kor	15th November	North-west of road Abazai—Shabkadr—Michni
Operations against the Mahsuds (2nd March–10th August, 1917.)	...	Defence of Sarwekai	2nd–8th March	*
		Affair of the Gwalerai Pass	9th April–1st and 16th May	The Gumal between Nili Kach and Kajuri Kach (both exclusive).
		Action of Kharkhwasta	9th–10th May	The route between the Khuzma Post and Sarwekai.
		Actions in the Shahur Valley	19th–24th June	The Shahur Valley above Haidari Kach, Nanu and the Khaisora.

Baluchistan.

Kalat Operations (i.) 1st June–10th July, 1915	...	...	...	
(ii.) 5th June–18th August, 1918	...	Affair of Wadh	25th June	South of Mastung.
Operations against the Marri and Khetran tribes (18th February–8th April, 1918.)	...	Defence of Gumbaz Post	19th–20th February	*
		Affair of Fort Munro	15th March	*
		Capture of the Hadb Position	6th April	*

† Up to the end of the Third Afghan War (8th August, 1919).

INDIA—*continued.*

THE THIRD AFGHAN WAR (6th May–8th August, 1919).

OPERATIONS.	BATTLES.		ACTIONS, &c.	MISCELLANEOUS INCIDENTS.	LIMITS.	
	NAME.	TACTICAL INCIDENTS INCLUDED.			CHRONOLOGICAL.	GEOGRAPHICAL.
Chitral Operations†	...	...	Capture of Arnawai	...	23rd–24th May	Kala Drosh (*exclusive*) to Narsai.
			Affair in the Bumboret Valley	...	17th July	The Bumboret Valley.
Khyber Operations†	...	...	Action of Bagh Springs	—*with subsequent* Occupation of Dakka	9th–11th May	The Khyber, north-west of Landi Kotal.
					13th May	*
			Affairs near Ali Masjid	...	15th and 16th May	The Khyber, between Fort Maude and Gurgura Post.
			Action of Dakka	...	16th and 17th May	North-west of Paindi Khakh.
			Affairs near Fort Maude	...	18th and 19th July	*
Kurram Operations†	...	...	Afghan Attack on Thal	...	28th–31st May	*
			Relief of Thal	...	30th May–3rd June	West of Doaba (*exclusive*).
			Affairs in the Upper Kurram	...	27th May–2nd June	The Kurram above Alizai.

47

			Evacuation of Militia Posts		
Waziristan and Derajat Operations†	...	...	...	25th-30th May	The Tochi Posts above Miran Shah and Spinwam line, and the South Waziristan Posts.
		Affair near Miran Shah	...	1st June	*
		Affair near Draband	...	3rd June	*
		Defence and Relief of Jandola	...	28th May-9th June	The route from Khirgi (exclusive) to Jandola.
Zhob Operations†	...	Withdrawal from Wana	...	25th-31st May	The route between Wana and Fort Sandeman.
		Affairs round Fort Sandeman	...	3rd June-14th July	
		Affair near Kapip	...	15th-17th July	The Lower Zhob.
		Affair of Hindu Bagh	...	22nd July	*
Chaman Operations†	...	Capture of Spin Baldak Fort	...	27th May	The road between Babar and Kapip.

† The period for all these operations is 6th May–8th August, 1919.

NORTH-EAST FRONTIER AND BURMA.

Punitive measures in the Kachin Hills (31st December, 1914–28th February, 1915.)	...	...	...	...	The area bounded on the north by latitude 26°30′, on the east by the River Mali Kha from where it cuts 26°30′ to the confluence, and thence the Irrawaddy until it cuts 25°15′. On the west longitude 96°. On the south latitude 25°. Eastern Boundary.—Left bank of Chindwin River. Southern Boundary.—Bargelai 23° 45″, west to longitude 93°. Western Boundary.—Longitude 93° to Lakhipur; thence adjoining Lakhipur to Manipur Road Station. Northern Boundary.—A line joining Manipur Road Station east to Tuzu River at point of junction 42 miles east by north from Kohima; thence follow river to junction with Chindwin. Troops at Kindat, Mawlaik and Monywa are also included.
Punitive measures in the Chin Hills (1st December, 1917–1st June, 1918.)	...	...	...	...	
Operations in the Kuki Hills (1st November, 1918–15th May, 1919.)	...	...	...	...	

RUSSIA.

MURMAN.

OPERATIONS.	BATTLES.		ACTIONS, &c.	MISCELLANEOUS INCIDENTS.	LIMITS.	
	NAME.	TACTICAL INCIDENTS INCLUDED.			CHRONOLOGICAL.	GEOGRAPHICAL.
Seizure of the Railway, 1918	...	...	...	Disarmament of the Bolsheviks as far as Soroki.	29th and 30th June	Kandalaksha and Kem.
Operations in Karelia, 1918	...	...	Capture of Ukhtinskaya	...	11th September	*
			Capture of Voknavolotskaya	...	21st September	*
			Action near Pyavozero Lake	...	3rd October	*
Winter Operations, 1918–19	...	...	...	Occupation of Bugozerski	16th January, 1919	West of the railway and south of Soroki.
			Capture of Segeja	...	18th February	South of the line Bugozerski—Kem—Sumski Posad.
			...	Transfer of troops to the Archangel front	February to April	The Soroki—Onega road beyond Sumski Posad.

Advance to Lake Onega, 1919	...	...	Capture of Urosozero	...	11th April	South of the line Bugozerski—Kem—Sumski Posad.
			Capture of Maselskaya	...	3rd May	
			Capture of Medvyejya Gora	Occupation of Povyeneta	18th May	South of the line Olimpi—Sumski Posad—Nyuhhotskoe.
				...	21st May	South of Maselskaya.
Lake Onega Operations, 1919	...	...	Capture of Kyapeselga	...	5th July	South of Maselskaya.
			Flotilla Actions	...	5th June, 3rd July, 2nd and 28th August.	Lake Onega.
Operations to cover withdrawal, 1919.	...	...	Action of Svyatnavolotski	...	27th August	South of Maselskaya.
			Capture of Lijma	...	14th–16th September	
				The Evacuation	1st–12th October	Murmansk and Kem.

RUSSIA—continued.

ARCHANGEL.

OPERATIONS.	BATTLES.		ACTIONS, &c.	MISCELLANEOUS INCIDENTS.	LIMITS.	
	NAME	TACTICAL INCIDENTS INCLUDED.			CHRONOLOGICAL.	GEOGRAPHICAL.
Seizure of the White Sea ports and Initial Advances (July–October, 1918.)	...	...	Capture of Archangel	...	1st and 2nd August	Mudyug Island to Archangel.
			Affair of Chunovakaya	...	3rd August	The Onega—Obozerskaya road.
			Affair of Puchuga	...	24th August	The Drina above Seletski.
			Affairs about Obozerskaya	...	31st August and 4th September	The Vologda railway south of the Kenza river.
			Actions of Chamova	...	12th–14th September	The Drina above Bereznik (exclusive).
			Affairs on the Yemtsa River	...	16th and 28th–30th September	The Yemtsa above the confluence of the Tyugra.
			Affair of Seletski	...	11th October	The Drina above Tulgas (exclusive).
			Affairs near Chekuevo	...	12th–17th October	The Onega above Chekuevo.
Defensive Operations, 1918–19 (October–August.)	...	...				
(a.) *On the Onega River and the Vologda Railway*	...	...	Affair of Kleshevo	...	27th December	The Onega above Chekuevo.
			Affairs near Bolshi Ozerki	...	17th March – 18th April	*
			Defence of Bolshi Ozerki	...	22nd–23rd July	*

(b.) *Between the Vologda Railway and the Drina River*	...	...	Affair at Tarasovo	...	25th and 29th January	* Between Kodish and Avdinskaya.
			Attack on Kodish	...	7th February	*
			Defence of Sredmekhrenga	...	8th–11th February	
(c.) *On the Dvina and Vaga Rivers*	...	...	Affair of Tulgas	...	11th–13th November	The Dvina above Chamova.
			Defence of Shenkursk	...	16th–25th January	The Vaga above Bereznik (exclusive).
			Affairs round Vistavka	...	1st–4th and 8th–10th March	The Vaga above Bereznik (exclusive).
			Affair of Ignatyevskoe	...	29th June	The Vaga above Bereznik.
(d.) *On the Pinega River*	...	...	First Affair of Ust-Pocha	...	1st–3rd June	The Pinega above Pinega.
Operations to cover withdrawal (August–September, 1919.)	...	BATTLE OF TROITSA	...	...	10th August	The Dvina above Troitsa.
			Affair of Yemtsa	...	29th–31st August	The Vologda Railway south of Obozerskaya.
			Second Affair of Ust-Pocha	...	4th September	The Pinega above Pinega.
				The Evacuation	27th September	Archangel.

RUSSIA—continued.

SIBERIA.†

OPERATIONS.	BATTLES.		ACTIONS, &c.	MISCELLANEOUS INCIDENTS.	LIMITS.	
	NAME.	TACTICAL INCIDENTS INCLUDED.			CHRONOLOGICAL.	GEOGRAPHICAL.
Usuri Operations ... (8th–28th August, 1918.)	BATTLE OF DUKHOVSKAYA	...	...	...	23rd–24th August	Between the lesser Usuri River and Lake Khanka, north of Dukhovskaya.
Ufa Operations ... (October, 1918–June, 1919.)	...	...	...	...	October, 1918— June, 1919	

† Including the operations of Siberian forces in European Russia.

FAR EAST AND PACIFIC.

CHINA.

Siege of Tsing-Tau (23rd September–7th November, 1914.)	...	...	23rd September–7th November	*

AUSTRALASIA.

(Conquest of the German Pacific Possessions.)

Operations of the New Zealand Expeditionary Force. (14th–30th August, 1914.)	...	...	Occupation of Samoa	29th August	*
Operations of the Australian Naval and Military Expeditionary Force. (11th September–6th November, 1914.)	...	...	Affair of Herbertshöhe	12th September	*
			Surrender of the German Forces	21st September	Herbertshöhe.

EAST AFRICA.

I.—THE CAMPAIGNS OF 1914-16.

Northern and Eastern Areas.

OPERATIONS.	BATTLES.		ACTIONS, &c.	MISCELLANEOUS INCIDENTS.	LIMITS.	
	NAME.	TACTICAL INCIDENTS INCLUDED.			CHRONOLOGICAL.	GEOGRAPHICAL.
Defence of the Uganda Railway (August–October, 1914.)	...	...	... Affair of Tsavo Affair of Majareni Affair of Gazi	German Occupation of Taveta	15th August 6th September 23rd September 8th October	* * * *
First Invasion of German East Africa (2nd–8th November, 1914.)	...	...	Attack on Tanga Affair of Longido	... ...	2nd–5th November 3rd November	The port of Tanga. Neighbourhood of Mt. Longido, south of Tanga (exclusive).
Umba Valley Operations (10th December, 1914 – 8th February, 1915.)	...	...	Affair of Jasin	...	18th–19th January	The Umba Valley.
Victoria Nyanza Operations (August, 1914–July, 1916.)	...	...	Affairs on the Kagera River Capture of Bukoba	... Occupation of Mwanza	August, 1914–July, 1916 22nd–23rd June, 1915 14th July, 1916	South of the line Mharas—Kaeyage. * *
Operations covering the construction of the Voi—Taveta Railway (May, 1915–February, 1916.)	...	...	Affair of Mbuyuni Attack on Salaita Hill	... ...	14th July 12th February	West of Kampi ya Bibi (exclusive). West of Mbuyuni (exclusive).

Operation				Action		Date	Location
Kilimanjaro Operations (5th–21st March, 1916.)	...	...	...	Action of Latema Nek	...	11th–12th March	West of Serengeti Camp (exclusive) on the Taveta line of advance, and south of Longido (exclusive) on that line.
				Action of Kahe	...	21st March	
Kondoa Irangi Operations (3rd April–10th May, 1916.)	...	...	...	Capture of Kondoa Irangi	...	17th–19th April	South-west of Arusha.
				German Attack on Kondoa Irangi	...	9th–10th May	
Operations for the Northern Railway, and Pursuit to the Nguru Hills (18th May–24th June, 1916.)	...	...	...	Affair of German Bridge	...	30th May	South of the Ruvu (Pangani) River.
				Action of Mkaramo	...	9th June	
					Occupation of Handeni	19th June	
Operations for the Central Railway							
(a.) *Seizure of the Railway from Kilimatinde to Kilosa* (24th June–22nd August 1916.)	...	...	...	...	...	24th June – 22nd August	South of Kondoa Irangi (exclusive)
(b.) *Advance through the Nguru Hills to Morogoro* (5th–26th August, 1916.)	...	...	...	Affair of Matamoudo	...	10th–11th August	South of Msiha Camp (exclusive).
				Affairs on the Wami River	...	13th–17th August	
Clearing of the Uluguru Mountains (27th August–13th September, 1916.)	...	...	...	Affair of Kissaki	...	7th September	South of Central Railway (exclusive).
				Affair of Dutumi	...	11th–13th September	
				—*with subsequent* Affair of Kisangire	...	9th October	

EAST AFRICA—continued.

I.—THE CAMPAIGNS OF 1914-1916—continued.
Northern and Eastern Areas—continued.

OPERATIONS.	BATTLES.		ACTIONS, &c.	MISCELLANEOUS INCIDENTS.	LIMITS.	
	NAME.	TACTICAL INCIDENTS INCLUDED.			CHRONOLOGICAL.	GEOGRAPHICAL.
Coast Operations (January, 1915–December, 1916)	...	...	...	Seizure of Mafia Island	10th–12th Jan., 1915	*
				Destruction of the "Königsberg"	11th July, 1915	River Rufiji.
				Landing at Manza Bay	4th July, 1916	*
				Landing at Pangani	23rd July, 1916	*
				Landing at Sadani	1st August, 1916	*
				Landing at Bagamoyo	15th August, 1916	*
				Landings at Konduchi and Mesaui Bay	2nd September, 1916	*
				Occupation of Dar es Salaam	4th September, 1916	*
				Landings at Kilwa Kivinje and Kilwa Kisiwani	7th September, 1916	*
				Landings at Lindi, Sudi Bay, and Mikindani	13th–16th Sept., 1916	*

Southern and Western Areas.

Defence of the Nyasaland—Rhodesia Border (August, 1914–24th May, 1916.)	...	Affair near Karonga	...	9th September, 1914	*
		Defence of Abercorn	...	5th–9th September, 1914	*
		Defence of Fife	...	6th–27th December, 1914	
		Affair of Sphinxhaven	Destruction of the "Hermann von Wissmann"	30th May, 1915	*
		Defence of Saisi	...	28th–29th June and 26th July–2nd August, 1915	*
Operations on Lake Tanganyika (23rd December, 1915–March, 1916.)	...	Capture of the "Kingani"	...	26th December	Lake Tanganyika
		Sinking of the "Hedwig von Wissmann"	...	9th February	
Advance from the Nyasa—Tanganyika line (25th May–23rd June, 1916.)	...	...	Occupation of Neu Langenburg	27th May	*
			Occupation of Bismarckburg	8th June	*
			Occupation of Ubena	23rd June	*
Advance on Iringa (22nd June–10th September, 1916.)	...	First Affair of Malangali	Occupation of Iringa	24th July	*
Operations on the Buhuje (18th August–21st October, 1916.)	...	Affairs near Mkapire	...	29th August	*
				28th September and 30th October.	
Operations against the Tabora Force (8th October–26th November, 1916.)	...	Second Affair of Malangali	...	8th–12th October	*
		Defence of Lupembe	...	12th–14th November	*
		Affairs about Ngominyi and Muhanga	...	19th–29th October	*
Operations in the Songea District (10th September–31st December, 1916.)	...	Capture of Ilembule	...	24th–26th November	*
		Defence of Songea	...	14th November	*

EAST AFRICA—continued.

II.—THE CAMPAIGNS OF 1917.

OPERATIONS.	BATTLES.		ACTIONS, &c.	MISCELLANEOUS INCIDENTS.	LISTS.	
	NAME.	TACTICAL INCIDENTS INCLUDED.			CHRONOLOGICAL.	GEOGRAPHICAL.
Advance to the Rufiji (December, 1916–January, 1917.)	...	...	Affairs about Kibata	...	6th–16th December, 1916.	*
			Affair of Wiranzi	...	1st January	*
			Action of Beho Beho	...	3rd–4th January	*
			Affair of Kibambawe	...	6th–7th January	*
			Capture of Mkindu	...	18th January	*
			Affair of Nyandete	...	24th January	*
Operations in the Kilwa and Lindi Areas, and advance to the Portuguese Frontier (April–November, 1917.)	...	...	Affair of Ngaura	...	18th April	*
			Affair of Lutende	...	30th June	*
			Affair of Mnindi	...	6th July	*
			Action of Narungombe	...	19th July	*
			Affair of Tandamuti	...	3rd August	*
			Affair of Narunyu	...	18th August	*
			Affair of Bwebo Chini	...	22nd September	*
			Action of Nyangao	...	16th–19th October	*
			Affair of Lukuledi	...	21st October	*
			Affairs round Chiwata	...	6th–18th November	*
				Surrender of Tafel's Force	28th November	The Mwiti Valley

Operations in the Songea District and advance on Liwale and Mahenge (1st January–13th November, 1917.)	...	Capture of Likuyu	...	24th January
		Affairs near Kitanda	...	22nd–30th January
		Affairs on the Likuyu-Mponda Road	...	6th July–1st October
		Affair of Likasa	Occupation of Tunduru	23rd August
				30th August
		Affairs of Kalimoto‡ and Mtriba‡	...	11th and 22nd Sept.
			Occupation of Mahenge‡	9th October
			Occupation of Liwale	29th October
		Affair at Ligundulu's	...	1st–2nd November
Pursuit and capture of Wintgens and Naumann (10th February–1st October, 1917.)	...	Affair of Tandala	...	19th–21st February
		Affair of St. Moritz	...	21st March

† Called in German accounts "Mahiwa."　　‡ Belgian forces.

III.—THE CAMPAIGN IN PORTUGUESE EAST AFRICA, 1918.

Operations in Portuguese Nyasa (11th January–23rd May, 1918.)	...	Affair of Nakote	...	5th May
		Affair of Korewa	...	22nd May
Operations in the Mozambique District (24th May–6th September, 1918.)	...	Affair of Nyamakura	...	1st–3rd July
		Affair of Nyamirue	...	21st–23rd July
		Affair of Nyamaroi	...	24th August
		Affair of Lioma	...	30th–31st August
Pursuit into Rhodesia (7th September–25th November, 1918.)	...	Affair of Mpwera	...	6th September
		Affair of Kayambi	...	6th November
		Surrender of the German Forces		25th November　Abercorn.

SOUTH-WEST AFRICA.

OPERATIONS.	BATTLES.		ACTIONS, &c.	MISCELLANEOUS INCIDENTS.	LIMITS.	
	NAME.	TACTICAL INCIDENTS INCLUDED.			CHRONOLOGICAL.	GEOGRAPHICAL.
Orange River Operations (20th August–10th November, 1914.)	...	...	Affairs near Raman's Drift	...	14th–27th September	North-east of Steinkopf (*exclusive*).
			Affair of Kaimoes	...	22nd October	The Orange river between Upington and Schuit Drift.
			Affair of Kakamas	...	24th October	
			—*with subsequent* Defence of Upington	...	23rd–24th January	
Southern Operations (15th September, 1914–30th April, 1915.)	...	...	...	Landing at Lüderitz Bay	19th September	
			...	Occupation of Aus	30th March	East of Chauknib.
			Action of Gibeon	...	25th–28th April	North of Beersheba (*exclusive*).
Northern Operations (31st December, 1914–9th July, 1915.)	...	...	...	Occupation of Swakopmund	14th January	
(i.) *Advance on Windhuk* (*22nd February–20th May.*)			Actions of Jakalswater	...	20th March	East of Swakopmund.
			Affair of Trekkopjes	...	26th April	
			...	Occupation of Windhuk	13th May	
(ii.) *Advance on Otavifontein* (*19th June–9th July.*)			Capture of Otavifontein	...	1st July	North of the Elefantsberg.
			...	Surrender of the German Forces	9th July	

WEST AFRICA.

TOGO.

Advance to Kamina... (8th–26th August, 1914.)	...	...	Affair of Agbeluvoe Affair of Khra	... ... Surrender of the German Forces	15th–16th August 22nd–23rd August 26th August	} North of Lome (exclusive). Amuchu.

FRENCH WEST AFRICA.*

Tuareg Operations ... (5th January–15th May, 1917.)	...	...	...	...	...	Beyond the Nigerian Frontier.

* Operations of Nigerian forces in French territory.

WEST AFRICA—continued.

CAMEROONS.

OPERATIONS.	BATTLES.		ACTIONS, &c.	MISCELLANEOUS INCIDENTS.	LIMITS.	
	NAME.	TACTICAL INCIDENTS INCLUDED.			CHRONOLOGICAL.	GEOGRAPHICAL.
Northern Operations (August–September, 1914.)	...	...	Affair of Tepe	...	25th August	On the Benue river in German territory.
			First Attack on Garua	...	29th–31st August	
			Affairs at Kuseri †	...	25th August and 29th September.	
			First Attack on Mora	...	27th August	On the Cross river in German territory.
			Affair of Nsanakang	...	6th September	
Duala Operations (September–November, 1914.) including *The first advances up the Northern and Midland Railways (29th September–15th November.)*	...	...	Capture of Duala	...	26th–27th September	
			Capture of Yabasi	...	14th October	
			...	Occupation of Edea†	26th October	North and east of Duala (exclusive).
			Capture of Buea and of the Cameroon Mountain.	Occupation of Mayuka	13th November	
					14th–15th November	
Operations up the Northern Railway (3rd December, 1914–4th March, 1915.)	...	...	Capture of Chang	...	3rd February	North of Majuka (exclusive).
			Affair of M'bureba	...	3rd February	
			Affair of Harmann's Farm	...	4th March	
The German Counter-Offensive (January, 1915.)	...	...	Defence of Edea	...	6th January, 1915	*
Coast Operations, 1914–15	...	...	...	At Kribi	19th December	*
				At Kampo	8th July	*
				At Nyong	13th July	*

First Advance on Yaunde ... (12th April–28th June, 1915.)	...	...	Affair of Ngwe	...	14th April
			Affair of Sendet	...	3rd–4th May
			First Affair of Wum Biagas	...	3rd–4th May	East of Edea (exclusive).
Operations for the Central Plateau (29th May–31st December, 1915.)	...	...	Capture of Garua	...	31st May–10th June
			Capture of Ngaundere	...	28th June
			Capture of Bamenda	...	22nd October
			Capture of Banyo	...	4th–6th November
			Capture of Fumban	...	2nd December	South-east of the Nigerian frontier.
Blockade of Mora ... (8th September, 1915–18th February, 1916.)	...	...	Second Attack on Mora	...	8th–9th September
			Third Attack on Mora	...	30th October – 4th November
				Capitulation of Mora	18th February
Second Advance on Yaunde ... (22nd September–31st December, 1915.)	...	...	Second Affair of Wum Biagas	...	9th October
			Affair at Lesog's	...	27th November
			Affair of Chang Mangas	...	17th December
			Affair of Mangelet	...	21st December
			...	Occupation of Yaunde†	1st January	South of the Sanaga River (exclusive)
—with subsequent —Pursuit to the Spanish frontier ... (1st January–17th February, 1916.)	...	...	...	...	1st January – 17th February

† French forces.

www.ingramcontent.com/pod-product-compliance
Lightning Source LLC
Chambersburg PA
CBHW081508090426
42743CB00015B/3138